THE SLOW MIRACLE OF TRANSFORMATION

By Mary Lou Wallner

The Slow Miracle of Transformation

3rd Edition – Revised and Updated

Cost: $15.00 (plus $2.00 shipping and handling)

ISBN 0-9740328-08

1st Printing–Feb 2003, 2nd Printing–Mar 2003, 3rd Printing– Oct 2005

Cover design by Christine Patterson-Zabielski
Edited and proofread by Donna Keel

All Scripture quotations are from the New International Version of the Bible unless otherwise noted.

For orders, information, reprint permission or to schedule a speaking engagement visit

the **TEACH Ministries** web site:
www.teach-ministries.org or call 1.501.542.4302

Other materials available from TEACH Project

Anna's Songs

A collection of songs written, composed and performed by Anna. *(See **Appendix A** of this book for lyrics)*

CD: $10.00 (plus $2.00 shipping and handling)

From Tragedy To Transformation

A 30-minute Video of Mary Lou's talk at Cathedral of Hope, Dallas, TX – Mother's Day 2003

VHS or **DVD:** $20.00 (plus $2.00 shipping and handling)

Family Stories: Journeys of Spirit in Mixed-orientation Families

A 35-minute Video featuring Mary Lou's story and Roberta Kreider's story with an introduction by the Reverend Peter Gomes of Harvard University

VHS or **DVD:** $20.00 (plus $2.00 shipping and handling)

DEDICATION

This book is dedicated to every conservative Christian
who has been taught to reject gay people
and to ban them from church life...
...and to every gay person who has felt the pain of rejection
and exclusion, not only from the church
but also from family and friends

TABLE OF CONTENTS

ACKNOWLEDGMENTS

I would like to thank my family for the love and support they have given me since Anna took her life. They have been very kind and compassionate.

I would like to thank my dear friend, Linda, for being such a wonderful support to me in every way since Anna's death. She has faithfully kept in touch with me, grieved with me, encouraged me and has stuck with me through thick and thin. She is an incredible lady!

I want to thank my counselor, Steve Sherbondy, for his wise counsel over the years. He has helped me with my talks and speaking engagements; he has been my mentor, and he has truly been my cheerleader.

Randy McCain, pastor of Open Door Community Church in Sherwood, Arkansas, put me in touch with David Plunkett and Timothy Malfo in Denver, Colorado. They graciously offered to print the first editions of this book, and I am grateful beyond words. Without these three incredibly special men, this book would not exist.

Mel White and Gary Nixon invited me to Lynchburg in October 1999. Without that experience, this book would not be a reality. They have given me something to live for.

I would like to thank Roby Sapp who came to live with us for six weeks in 2001. The purpose was for her to come out of the closet and learn to be open and comfortable with who she is, a Christian who just happens to be a lesbian. She taught me much about myself, and about life in general. I had the joyous privilege of introducing her to Dotti Berry. In an email from Roby, she says, "I can't ever thank you enough for listening to God when he/she gave you the 'message' that maybe we should date. I love this woman more each day and I feel so blessed to have her in my life. Words cannot express how grateful I am. Thank you for being the messenger, and delivering a message to both of us that has changed our lives forever. We will forever be grateful for your presence, and your influence in our lives…and your friendship." What a gift these two women are to me.

Thank you—the readers—for being willing to take the plunge and read this book. My prayer is that it will minister to you in a very special way.

There are no adequate words to express my love and appreciation for my wonderful husband, Bob, for all his loving support, patience, and valuable advice as I have worked on this book. I could not have done it without him. He is a very bright light in my life, and this is as much his project as it is mine.

And last, and most importantly, I want to express my thankfulness to God for the way He has worked in my life, especially in the past eight years. He has never failed me. He has never left me and He has never forsaken me. The gift of His Son, Jesus Christ, makes my life possible.

FOREWORD

Foreword by the Reverend Dr. Mel White,
Executive Director of Soulforce

WWW.SOULFORCE.ORG

In the Torah (Genesis 9) God made a promise to Noah, a covenant written across the skies in a bow of many colors, that the Creator would not flood the world again. Since ancient times the rainbow has been a symbol of God's desire to protect and preserve creation. In the following pages, Mary Lou Wallner celebrates two new rainbows that appeared unexpectedly in her life with the dawn of her own long, dark night of the soul.

The first rainbow she celebrates is a symbol of the second chance to life that God has given her after the storm of grief and guilt that followed her daughter's self-inflicted death.

But Mary Lou's rainbow also symbolizes the lesbian, gay, bisexual, and transgender community of faith who surrounded her with love and forgiveness even as she remained convinced that their sexual orientation was both a "sickness" and a "sin."

It may be a risk to read this dramatic, deeply moving, moment-by-moment story of the transformation of a mother whose ignorance helped lead to her own daughter's death.

You may find yourself being forced to leave the "safe place" where the issue of homosexual orientation had been neatly settled, to find yourself facing an avalanche of questions that you've never really asked.

That storm of questions is currently raging across America's Catholic and Protestant Churches, dividing families, splitting congregations, and destroying lives. Is homosexuality a "sickness" that can and should be healed, a "sin" that needs to be forgiven, a "lifestyle" that needs to be forsaken?

On one side are psychologists, psychiatrists, scientists, historians, schoolteachers, administrators and counselors who say, "No. That debate has been settled by the scientific and historical facts."

On the other side are religious leaders who quote six Bible passages to say, "Yes. Any authority who disagrees with our biblical understanding is wrong."

Must we, as people of faith who love and honor the Bible, continue to ignore the scientific, psychological, psychiatric, medical and historical evidence? Is our understanding of those six Bible verses used to condemn sexual and gender minorities more trustworthy, more important to us, more conclusive than the lives of those we love...even the lives of our own children?

Until her daughter's suicide, Mary Lou Wallner was content to trust (and even quote) those anti-homosexual church teachings even if it meant ignoring her daughter's desperate pleas for understanding. But with Anna's death, Mary Lou and her husband, Bob, began a journey into the truth about sexual orientation that changed their lives forever.

If you read this tear-stained, hope-saturated journal, it will change your life as well. It could even save your life or the life of someone you love. I'm not exaggerating. Mary Lou learned the hard way that religious teachings can be tragically off the mark. Now she understands the terrible reality that sincere people who quote the Bible can be sincerely wrong. When that happens, instead of using God's Word to bring life, they bring intolerance, suffering and even death.

For two thousand years Christian priests and pastors, bishops, cardinals, and popes have misunderstood and misused the biblical texts to support injustice and intolerance. The Bible has been quoted to justify bloody crusades and fiery inquisitions, slavery, apartheid, and segregation, the second-class-citizenship of women and children, and now the current anti-homosexual crusade.

If you are a parent of a lesbian or gay, bisexual or transgender child and you hold blindly to the notion that homosexuality is a choice; if you believe sincerely that homosexuals can and must be changed by reparative, ex-gay or transformational therapy; if you have been convinced that your gay child has made a tragic, sinful choice and/or needs counseling to "overcome" his or her mental illness, beware! The lives of those you love are at risk. Ask Mary Lou Wallner. She quoted those biblical texts to her daughter, Anna, and the consequences were catastrophic.

Unfortunately, Anna's story is all too common. Suicide has become a common cause of death to lesbian, gay, bisexual, and transgender people, especially those who are raised by parents who quote the verses that are currently being misused to caricature and condemn gay people.

In 1989, A Report of the Secretary's Task Force on Youth Suicide, by the

Department of Health and Human Services, ignited a controversy that continues to the present day. In the chapter on gay and lesbian youth suicide, the author estimated that "gay youth are two to three times more likely to attempt suicide than other young people."

Religious leaders refused to consider the evidence, let alone to acknowledge that their teachings were in large part responsible for the death of God's gay children. They insisted that the Report was based on faulty data and research bias.

Nine years later, an extensive study by researchers at the University of Minnesota (published in the August, 1998 edition of the *American Journal of Public Health*) demonstrated that homosexual or bisexual junior high school and senior high school boys are seven times more likely than heterosexual boys of the same age to report suicide attempts.

The study utilized data from a 1987 survey of more than 36,000 Minnesota students in grades seven to twelve. The survey was filled out by 95 percent of the students. Researchers from the University's Youth and AIDS Project said their "unbiased" findings "end contentions over whether there is a relationship between homosexuality and suicide."

According to the American Association of Suicidology, studies traditionally demonstrate that females are up to nine times more likely to attempt suicide than males. Males, though, are six times more likely to complete a suicide (usually because they have easier access to guns than do their female counterparts). The University of Minnesota findings placed heterosexual girls in the 14 percent range for reported suicide attempts. About 20 percent of homosexual or bisexual teenage girls responded similarly.

There has not been a study of gay or lesbian suicides to determine the role in these deaths played by pastors, priests, or parents who misused Leviticus 20 or Romans 1 to condemn their own children, but the circumstantial evidence is overwhelming.

I could tell true stories of dozens of gay and lesbian youth and adults from Christian homes who killed themselves for one reason: They could not believe that God loved them as they were. They heard so many times that they were "sick" and "sinful" that they began to believe it. They tried hard to change what God had created in them, and when they could not change, they became guilty, depressed and suicidal.

Here's the full text of an email we received that Mary Lou quotes briefly in her book.

> It is with a great sense of anger, frustration, and sadness that I write to let you know of a death in our Christian family, experienced directly by one of our community members. C.H. received word earlier this week that her 28-year-old nephew, Mark, hung himself. He was a gay man. He accepted his sexuality until he became a Christian a few months ago. Understanding from the Bible and the Church that he could not be both a Christian and a gay man, Mark's suicide note addressed to God read, 'I don't know how else to fix this.'

In 2001, Soulforce volunteers stood in prayerful protest in St. Peter's Square directly beneath the Pope's Vatican window holding up pictures of Alfredo Ormando, a young Catholic writer who burned himself to death to protest the antigay teachings of his beloved Church. In the last page of his diary, Alfredo writes:

> Monday night I'll depart for Rome by bus. Tuesday morning I'll be in San Pietro… They will think I'm a lunatic because I chose the Vatican to set myself on fire. I hope they'll understand the message I want to leave: it is a form of protest against the Church that demonizes homosexuality—and at the same time all of nature, because homosexuality is a child of Mother Nature.

Benny Hill, a young gay Christian in San Antonio, Texas, hanged himself in his grandmother's garage after the Christian Coalition published his name in the local paper for being arrested with other gay men who had gathered in a local park. Benny's sister and brother-in-law asked me to conduct a memorial service in front of the newspaper office that agreed to publish the report that lead to his death.

Almost ten years ago, a young lesbian emailed me this brief message: "If you can prove that God loves me as I am, I won't kill myself." For three days I emailed answers to every question she asked. On the fourth day, there was no response. On Monday, her parents emailed me the tragic news. "Our daughter killed herself on Wednesday night. We found copies of your emails on her desk. She had written, 'Please write to Dr. White and tell him thanks. His messages meant so much to me, but he came into my life too late.'"

When will the suffering end? How many lesbians and gays named Anna, Orlando, Mark or Benny have to die before religious leaders have the courage to quit making outcasts out of God's gay children and welcome them at last into full and unqualified membership?

As you read Mary Lou's courageous confession, as you page through her deeply moving cry for understanding, as her words sneak past your defenses and open you heart to new truth, gay or straight, you will also hear the still small voice of God saying, "Whoever you are, remember always that I created you and I love you exactly as you are."

INTRODUCTION

It has been eight years since I committed my beautiful 29-year-old daughter to the cold, hard ground in Springfield, Missouri. I find myself wondering what her body looks like now. Morbid thought! It has probably decayed, and we did not purchase a sealed casket, so maybe bugs or mildew have seeped into the vault.

I never understood why people went to cemeteries to visit the graves of their loved ones. I figured if the deceased person was a Christ-follower, that person was really not there anyway. They were in heaven. So why would a person want to visit a place where their beloved family member or friend was not? But, since Anna died, I understand.

Her grave and tombstone are over 200 miles from where I live. If they were closer, I would go often. There's something about being there that allows me to "connect" with her just a bit, and that comforts me. It always makes me cry—maybe because seeing my daughter's name, birthday and death date artistically engraved into black granite convinces me that this is *real*. This *happened*. It happened to *me*. My heart screams "NO-O-O-O!"

The first words my younger daughter spoke to me upon finding out about her sister's death were, "Mom, you can't blame yourself. It's not your fault." She seemed almost desperate to know that I wouldn't play the "blame-game." But how could I *not*? We have all heard the proverbial story in which a husband and a wife have a fight just before he leaves for work. Then he gets killed in a car accident on the way to the office. One of the worst aspects of losing Anna was that she had written me a letter almost seven months prior to her death severing all ties with me. How could I cope with the *way* our relationship ended?

In 1977, Anna's dad and I were divorced. I grew up in a Christian home and divorce was not acceptable. I could not believe it when it happened to me, knowing again, that I was largely to blame. I thought *this has to be the worst* hit *I could ever take in life!* Little did I know what was to come.

I started journaling about Anna's death a week after she died, but I could not make it public until now. There have been (and sometimes still are) times when I did not think I could go on living with the pain. Many days, I simply wanted to follow Anna. But now, I have lived eight full years since her death. It seems like some sort of milestone. Do I miss her any less? No way! Do I cry as much? Almost.

Over the past eight years, I have had plenty of doubts and questions about whether I actually *would* or *could* survive this. I had accepted Christ as my Savior at the age of ten but I was not sure if the God *I* knew was big enough for this one. Have I asked God *why?* Only about a trillion times. Has He answered me? No! …or has He?

I am slowly and painfully learning to admit the truth about *me*. I screwed up royally. I have made terrible, hurtful, and sinful choices. I have had to look at the ways I contributed to Anna's death. The most painful thing I have ever done is to go back in time and actually work at *figuring out* what I did that led Anna down this path. I was pretty sure God would forgive me, but Anna was not able to do this. I think I knew on some level for many years that I had failed as a mother in countless ways. But did I go to Anna and confess my sin? No. I simply criticized her for being gay, while I continued to live in the pit of denial about my own problems. Sometimes I think Christians are the only people who shoot their wounded. I *shot* Anna when she announced, "I want to be gay" in a letter to me received right before Christmas in 1988.

Now, I was facing the worst tragedy of my life. I had never lost a close family member until Anna took her life. Of course, I assumed that my first family loss would be my parents. (My Dad passed away on his 88th birthday in January of 2000.) Never in a million years did I dream my first family death would be my daughter. That is all backwards. Our children are not supposed to die before we do. This was all so wrong.

At times, I find it very hard to remember that *nothing* passes through the grid of God's will and on to me without Him knowing about it or allowing it to happen. Job 1:22 says it well: "The Lord said to Satan, 'Very well, then, everything [Job] has is in your hands, but on the man himself do not lay a finger.'"

I have two signs on my refrigerator. One says:

> *Dear Mary Lou,*
> *Trust Me. I have everything under control.*
> *Love, Jesus*

The other says:

Dear Mary Lou,
I will be handling all your problems today.
I will not need your help, so have a good day.
Love, God

Could I actually do this? Would I ultimately be able to trust Him in this?

I

THE END

CHAPTER ONE

Day One—February 28, 1997

THE PHONE CALL

Suicide is deadly. Did you know that one person, per minute, attempts suicide in the United States, and that 84 people complete it every day?

It was Friday about 10:00 p.m., February 28, 1997. Bob, my husband of 20 years, and I were sitting on the couch eating popcorn and watching TV—our normal Friday night tradition. Bob (who retired from architectural practice in July 1996) had been on the phone with a former co-worker, who had been fired after 30 years of service. Bob finished his conversation about 9:45 p.m. We were getting ready to watch the news and indulge in another Friday night tradition—non-fat frozen yogurt.

The phone rang. Bob answered it, and I heard him say, "Hi, Nathan." Nathan is my ex-husband and the father of my two daughters. Silence. Then I heard an unfamiliar noise come from Bob, like he'd just been punched in the stomach and had the wind knocked out of him. He sat down on a chair near the phone. His conversation with Nathan lasted less than two minutes, but I knew something was wrong. I had a sick feeling in the pit of my stomach, like "butterflies," but precipitated by fear rather than anxiety. My heart jumped into my throat. By the time Bob got off the phone, I knew what the conversation was about. I could not take it in.

Bob had a contorted, painful expression on his face. He looked stricken! I said, "It's Anna, isn't it?" Bob nodded. "She's dead, isn't she?" Bob nodded again. "Did she commit suicide?" For the third time, Bob nodded, and held me. I closed my eyes tightly, and said, "No, no, no, no, no, no, no," over and over again. I could not open my eyes. Maybe if I kept my eyes closed, it would not be true. If I opened them, it would be.

Bob said that I could call Anna's dad back, when I was ready to find out the details of my daughter's death. My 29-year-old Masters-degreed social worker, brilliant and musically talented daughter was dead. This could not be happening. This was not real. I would awaken any moment from this terror-filled nightmare and find that Anna was still alive, though still very troubled. These kinds of things only happened to *other* people, not to *me*. I was a Christian. These kinds of things do not happen to Christians.

Anna was a Christian. Christians do not commit suicide, do they? My mind could not take it all in. I was numb, in shock.

I did not wake up from this nightmare. I was not asleep. This was *real*, and it *was* happening to me. I gathered my courage to make a call to Nathan, Anna's dad. I was not crying. I was nearly catatonic. I wondered what I had done to cause this. It had to be my fault, somehow. Since that time, many have said the same words to me that my younger daughter, Beckie, said that February evening. "Mom, it's not your fault. You cannot blame yourself. You did the best you could." Those words did carry a grain of truth, as I did not *willfully* injure Anna emotionally. But, over all, it was just not true.

Of course, I have made the same comments to others. Why? If any of my girlfriends confessed her child's rebellion to me, or talked about her "prodigal" child, and if I had even the tiniest inkling that my girlfriend had contributed to her child's errant ways, then I would have to admit the same to be true for myself. In my past, I could not do that. It has taken nearly thirty years to admit that I made *terrible mistakes.* That acknowledgment feels awful.

In countless ways, I have tried to run from those feelings. The voices in my head and voices from others, made it so easy for me to "pass the buck." Voices that said, "If you can't control it, you're not responsible for it." Voices that said, "You did the best you could." Even more voices, that said, "She was old enough to make her own choices." Sometimes, during the past six years, as I have discovered more about Anna's life, I felt I actually murdered her. I did not. Her death was her decision. That final act was hers, alone. Did I create an atmosphere, as she was growing up, that led her to such a desperate act? You bet! I will *never* be off the hook on that one.

Dr. Paul Dickson, in a message at Bibletown, in Boca Raton, Florida, said that when a person dies in an accident, there is a sense of tragedy; when a person dies of a terminal illness, there is a sense of sorrow. When a person is murdered, there is a sense of horror. But, when a person dies of suicide, there is a sense of *utter failure.* How true I have found this to be!

Anna's dad and I were divorced in 1977, soon after moving from St. Louis to Colorado. Nathan wanted to go to seminary. We had a difficult marriage, at best. We had years of counseling—it seemed like decades. You name it—psychiatrists, psychologists, pastors, marriage counselors, we'd seen them all! At times, we both thought we could make our marriage work. In 1976, Nathan quit his job as a purchasing agent for a large St. Louis corporation, and we moved to Colorado so he could attend seminary.

That move was probably the hardest thing I had ever done, at least at that point in my life. I did not want to move. I felt like I had finally "arrived!" I was living in a gorgeous, two-story brick home—three bedrooms, four bathrooms, and two fireplaces. We lived in the same neighborhood where I had grown up, and my children were going to the same elementary school I had attended. My parents lived two miles away, and were truly our best friends. I did not work full time. Nathan was a good provider. I started a ladies Bible study, which met in my home weekly. We had an evening Bible study, with many of these same women and their husbands. Many came to know the Lord. We were active in a wonderful Baptist church nearby. I agreed to move because I knew Nathan was not happy in his job and wanted to be trained in his gift of preaching.

We settled in a four-room apartment. I went to work for a local physician, and Nathan went to seminary, working nights as a security guard in our apartment complex. Soon, our marriage was in trouble. Nathan had difficulty trusting me, and with reason some of the times. On numerous occasions, I was emotionally unfaithful to Nathan. For many years, he believed I had been sexually unfaithful. I had not. I made some terrible choices. Something snapped in me, after one particular blow-up. I said, "Nathan, get your act together, or get out. I can't live like this anymore. You don't trust *anybody,* not even God." That night, he left. It was January 13, 1977.

I met Bob through my job, soon after Nathan left. I fell for him. Bob became my husband, and 25 years later, I still love him deeply.

What does all this have to do with Anna's suicide? Divorce has serious, ongoing consequences, although God does forgive the act of divorce. Our divorce had a deadly effect on Anna. She was nine years old, and she was very mature for her age. I began to rely on her for comfort, too much. Dan Allender, in his book, *The Wounded Heart,* says, "The role distortion tears away a child's childhood and replaces it with adult burdens that are too heavy to lift, but must be carried if the child is to enjoy any benefits of life or love in the dysfunctional home. The forsaking of childhood begins the long process of giving up the soul in order to taste a few crumbs of life" (Pp. 75-75).

After the divorce, and my marriage to Bob, Anna began to withdraw emotionally from me. She looked for nurturing elsewhere. In retrospect, I probably would have done the same thing if I had been her. Anna looked for love from older men, but more often from older women (teachers, neighbors, etc.). She became very attached to these people, and I was so enthralled with my new husband that I just let her go. She was out of my hair. I later wondered if this had anything to do with her homosexuality, or was she simply born with a homosexual orientation?

On that Friday evening, February 28, 1997, I finally gathered a shred of brainpower and called Nathan back. In a whispering voice, I asked, "How did she do it?" Nathan told me that Anna had hung herself in her apartment, from the closet bar, using her dog's leash. My mind reeled. I did not have a closet bar that would support my own weight, and Anna weighed more than I did. How could this happen?

J.W., a friend of Anna's, found her. He lived in the same apartment complex as she, and cared very much for her. J.W. had asked Anna to marry him. They had put money down on a rental house, purchased a washer and dryer, and planned to move in together. Someone told us that Anna was only marrying J.W. because she wanted to have a baby!

Realizing my shock, numbness and confusion, Nathan supplied a few details for me. Questions he knew I'd think of later, but was too emotionally paralyzed to consider. He told me that the death certificate affixed the time of death as 12:30 a.m., February 28th. The cause of death? Asphyxiation. On the death certificate, in the box that reads "describe how injury occurred," the Medical Examiner had written, "self-induced asphyxiation with ligature." What in the world is a ligature? Webster says, "the act of tying, binding, or constriction." Another box on the death certificate, labeled "approximate interval between onset and death," had only one word written: "minutes."

I later learned, from the Springfield Deputy Medical Examiner, that a death by hanging is very quick and painless. This very kind gentleman told me that it only takes four pounds of pressure to occlude the carotid arteries on each side of the neck. This cuts off the blood supply to the brain. The victim is rendered unconscious in the first 15-20 seconds. Death follows about five to seven minutes after consciousness is lost. There is no air hunger, no feelings of suffocation, no clawing at the ligature around the neck to try to reverse the hanging. There simply is not enough time.

Nathan also told me that J.W. did not find Anna until about three or four o'clock the afternoon of February 28th. It was 8:00 p.m. when the sheriff and a chaplain arrived at Nathan's home and informed him. I cannot imagine what must have gone through his mind, when he saw a police officer at his door, and a man with a clerical collar.

Nathan supplied a bit more information about the events that took place February 28. He told me that Susan, Anna's friend (also a social worker), and loving partner of two-and-a-half years, had tried to page Anna all day. Anna had not responded to the page. Finally, about 4:00 p.m., Susan left her workplace and went to Anna's apartment. Susan found the entire area cordoned off with that yellow tape that tells you a tragedy has occurred. Numerous police officers and neighbors were there. Susan spent about two hours answering questions and giving information. Susan told the police how to contact Nathan, Anna's in-town next of kin.

About 10:45 p.m. February 28th, I had a brief conversation with my other daughter, Beckie. She wanted to be certain that I was not blaming myself for Anna's death. I hoped she was not condemning herself, either. At times like this, blame is irrelevant, but nevertheless, on everyone's mind. Later on, responsibility would become important.

We made two more phone calls before going to bed that night. We called some friends in Florida who had experienced this kind of pain. On January 3, 1996, John, their 29-year-old son, had taken his life by a gunshot wound to his head. I remember when we received that news. We were on our way to the airport to travel to Ixtapa, Mexico, for a week of sun, sand and surf. They sent us a letter that told of John's death and the funeral details. They did not say how John died. I guessed suicide, since I knew John had suffered from depression. I knew that those dear friends were the first people with whom we needed to talk. It was almost midnight in their Florida town, but I did not care. My daughter was dead. The irony was that John and Anna had grown up together for the first seven years of their lives. John was born just 362 days before Anna. Both John and Anna were 29 years old when they took their lives.

Rick and Patti were not in bed. I knew that I needed help, and quickly turned to this couple who had also experienced the wrenching tragedy of suicide. They were wonderful. I kept repeating, "I don't know what to do." I have always been a performance-based person and a "fixer," and it seemed as if there should be something I could *do* to "fix" this situation. There was not. I was no longer in control—of anything.

Patti was very helpful and encouraged us to have an open casket, just as they had done with John. Rick and Patti felt very strongly about this, even though John had shot himself in the head. The mortician was able to make his body presentable. They said this gave them some "closure." (I have learned to detest that word! How could the memory of my precious daughter ever be "closed out" of my mind? It could not, and I did not want it to.) There were several differences in the death acts of these two young people, other than the methods used. John had left a note, and a very clean apartment. Anna left no note, and a very messy apartment.

The other phone call we made was to the leaders of the small group we belonged to from our church. They were shocked, overwhelmed, and they promised to pray for us.

Bob and I readied ourselves for bed, although it was ludicrous to think we could sleep. Bob was to attend a men's church breakfast the next morning and was supposed to take a disabled friend. We did not know what to do about this. To make even the smallest decisions seemed insurmountable. We tried making other arrangements for this friend, but were unsuccessful. We both got out of bed at six the next morning, March 1st. We threw on some sweats, drove to this man's house, and gave him the tickets. We trusted that he would find a way to the church. He did.

We slept very little that night, just some fitful dozing. I kept repeating in my mind, "Anna is dead. Anna is dead. Anna is dead." *How* was I going to tell my 83-year-old mother and 85-year-old father? How was I going to tell my brother, my sister, and their families? Only God could figure that one out. I could not. Sleep eluded me.

CHAPTER TWO

Day Two—March 1, 1997

THE NEXT DAY

March 1st was cold and cloudy, with snow in the air. I had not even been to sleep. The black of night just became a little grayer. The pain in my heart became less numb, and hurt a lot more. I had to notify my family. How? I did not know. I always considered myself the "black sheep" of my family. At age 18, I left my family's Plymouth Brethren sect, a small, conservative and exclusive evangelical Christian group. I married someone outside that sect. I was divorced, and had a gay daughter, who had now committed suicide.

It seemed an impossible task to inform my family of this latest tragedy and personal failure. Somehow, I had to do it. Finally, I decided to call my brother, since he was the oldest of my siblings. I was not sure where he was. I thought he had been on vacation in Florida. I knew my parents were not home. They were probably in Charlotte, North Carolina, where my Dad was attending a church meeting.

My sister in Pennsylvania was having a retreat in her home. About 40 young people were in attendance. I first called my brother's daughter and son-in-law in Orlando, Florida, around 7:30 a.m., to locate my brother Dave. My nephew-in-law, Jim answered the phone. I blurted out that Anna had taken her life. I asked where my brother was. Jim said, "He's here." "Thank you, Lord," I thought.

Jim and his wife had adopted a Haitian boy who had arrived February 28th, the day Anna died. Jim called my brother to the phone, and told his wife, my niece, who started to scream in the background. She and Anna were nearly the same age, and at one time had been very close. I hurt for her.

My brother Dave just cried out over the phone, "Oh! Mary Lou!" He began to cry and told me how sorry he was. We got down to the business of deciding how to tell the rest of the family. Dave suggested that *he* tell Mother and Daddy, who were in Charlotte, North Carolina. We decided Dave would wait until later in the day, when my Dad's meeting was over. I would call my sister Marj, but would postpone the call until later because of the retreat.

Half an hour after we hung up, Dave called back. He and his family did not think it was a good idea to wait to tell the rest of the family. Dave had taken his oldest daughter, her husband, and their little girl to the Orlando airport to fly home to Chicago. The daughter had called from the airport, saying they had missed their flight. Dave, his wife, my niece and her family all drove back to the airport to tell my Chicago niece and her family about Anna.

My Dad was in the middle of his church meeting at a retirement home, and my Mother was at the retirement home administrator's own home. My cousin Barb was also at the meeting. My brother made sure Barb was with my Dad when he called. (Barb and my folks went to the same St. Louis church and were very close. Barb was Anna's piano teacher and babysat both my daughters when they were very young.) My brother Dave told my Dad about Anna over the phone, and the administrator's wife told my Mother. I cannot even bear to know what their reactions were.

My folks called me shortly afterward, and my Dad said, "The most wonderful thing you did for us was to put us in touch with Rick and Patti" (the friends whose son John had taken his life a year earlier). Earlier, in January, my folks took a trip to Florida to visit relatives. They had a few days to "kill" before going to Charlotte, North Carolina. I had suggested they visit Rick and Patti, whom they knew when we all lived in St. Louis. I thought it would be an encouragement for Rick and Patti to tell my folks about John's suicide. That is exactly what happened. My folks had lunch with Rick and Patti and heard the entire story of John's manic depression and suicide. This occurred just *four days* before their granddaughter Anna took her life. I remember having a "flash" of thankfulness to God. When I heard of this visit, I thought *what an amazing tapestry of relationships the Lord weaves when He is taking care of His own!* In God's great love and mercy, He had truly prepared my mother and father for this tragedy and heartache.

I then telephoned my sister. She just burst into tears. She had seen Anna more recently than I had.

It was March in Chicago, as only March in Chicago can be. I was in such a state of emotional upheaval and insecurity that I could not bear to be separated from Bob. We asked a neighbor to care for our cat while we were away. The neighbor just hugged me when I told her about Anna's suicide.

Bob drove me to my hairdresser's to get a scheduled perm that I needed. Judy, my Christian hairdresser, was wonderful. I was feeling guilty about doing something so mundane and frivolous as getting a perm. Judy made me feel I'd done the right thing, that I needed to look as good as possible, and not have to fuss with my hair. I am not sure why it mattered.

In the early afternoon, we arrived back home and made some more telephone calls to family and friends. Peter, my nephew, called to offer his love and sympathy. He and Anna had been very close during their growing up years. Anna and Susan had driven all night to go to Peter's wedding in March 1995. Peter said he would be at the funeral and would do whatever he could to help. He would speak, serve as a pallbearer, anything.

We talked to Nathan and his wife, Cheryl, and my daughter Beckie, several times that day. Nathan and Cheryl had picked a funeral home and a casket. They informed us of costs and options. We asked for a less expensive casket ($800 instead of $1200). The $1200 casket was sealed and we did not think that necessary since Anna was not there anyway. It was, and is, so very comforting to know that Anna accepted the Lord as her Savior at a very young age. She had lived an active Christian life, until we moved from Wyoming to Illinois in 1985. We are convinced that Anna is with the Lord. The words in John 10:27-28 have provided continual comfort: "My sheep listen to my voice, I know them, and they follow me. I give them eternal life, and they shall never perish; *no one can snatch them out of my Father's hand.*"

We talked a bit about whether to have Anna's casket open or closed. Nathan and Beckie were in favor of having a closed casket. I wanted it open. I decided to pray, although at that point my prayers were little more than "groans that words cannot express" (Romans 8:26b).

Nathan and Cheryl had purchased three cemetery plots in the same cemetery where Cheryl's mother is buried. They were willing to have Anna buried in the third lot (the other two were for themselves). I made only one request—to go to Anna's apartment and pick out the clothes for her to wear. It was not to be.

About 8:00 p.m. Saturday night, our church's (Willow Creek Community Church) small group leaders came to our home. We talked, and they prayed with us. This offered some measure of comfort.

I did almost all my packing while on the phone with friends who needed to know. It's a wonder I had any of the right clothing when we got to Springfield the next day. We tried to sleep before we left early Sunday morning. My doctor had been kind enough to prescribe medication to help me sleep. I did sleep some that night.

CHAPTER THREE

Day Three—March 2, 1997

THE JOURNEY

Sunday morning, March 2 was clear and cold. Bob and I left about 7:15 a.m. for Springfield. For some time, I read aloud from the Bible—passages that gave much comfort. Like Deuteronomy 33:27, which says, *"The eternal God is your refuge and underneath are the everlasting arms,"* and, II Corinthians 5:8-9 which says, *"We are confident, I say, and would prefer to be away from the body and at home with the Lord. So we make it our goal to please Him, whether we are at home in the body or away from it."* We listened to some worship music. I was amazed at our "calm." This may have been the first time *ever* that I felt the Lord's arms around me—almost physically. I knew He, and He alone, was comforting me, not other people that He was using—just my Savior. I wondered if this would continue. It did not. I remember saying to Bob, "I don't want Anna's death to be in vain." I did not realize what forms that wish would take.

Bob did most of the driving. We stopped at a Howard Johnson's outside St. Louis for lunch. I ate some soup, and we each had an ice cream cone with real ice cream—the first real ice cream in years. Bob had five-vessel coronary by-pass surgery in June 1995, and we had been trying to watch our fat intake since then. Suddenly, fat grams just did not seem to matter. Our daughter was dead.

About 4:30 p.m. Sunday, we arrived at Nathan's home in Springfield. I had asked Bob's permission to hug Nathan. Bob said, "Of course." When we arrived, there were hugs all around, and tears, and murmurs of "I'm sorry." We unloaded our things, and sat and talked awhile. Beckie, my daughter, and her husband Gary arrived shortly after we did. Their three-and-a-half-year-old son remained with other relatives.

Pastor Gary Hay, the minister that Nathan and Cheryl had chosen, arrived about 6:00 p.m. He was the pastor of the church they attended, and to us he was a gift from God. He came in, took off his coat, loosened his tie, accepted a cup of coffee and sat down in a rocking chair. He said, "Now, talk to me about Anna." He asked each of us to relate a good memory about her. We talked about Anna for almost two hours. Early in the conversation, I had asked this kind pastor if he knew the Lord as his

Savior. He gently smiled and said, "Yes, I do." I needed that assurance, since I don't believe being a pastor necessarily guarantees heaven. It was an uncomfortable question for me to ask. Since Anna's death, I have asked many "uncomfortable" questions, with no thought of how they might be perceived. Her death has given me a boldness I did not possess before. In the spotlight of Anna's death, it did not seem important what others would think.

When Pastor Gary heard about Anna's sexual orientation, he wondered if Anna was about to turn a corner into something so terrible she could not return from it. For about two years, I agreed with him. Now, I believe otherwise.

My mind and heart still screamed, "Why suicide? Why not let her be hit by a truck or something?" No answers came at that time. We talked about what we wanted at the funeral, and we told Pastor Gary we wanted the Gospel to be preached more than anything. He was very willing to do that.

During this two-hour discussion, my son-in-law Gary talked about his relationship with Anna. He remembered seeing her recently and asked her how she was doing. She replied, "I'm *so* tired." Why was Anna so tired? She was on disability for depression. I was later to suspect the origin of her fatigue.

My son-in-law Gary has experienced much loss in his life, including his own father's death. Pastor Gary asked him if he would like to say a few words at the funeral. He considered it, but decided not to, since Beckie did not want him away from her side during the funeral. I understood this. I did not want Bob away from me, either.

We talked with Pastor Gary about my Dad's recent encounter with Anna. My Dad had spent February 4th, with Anna, just 24 days before she died. Around Christmas, Anna asked my folks for money for her counseling (she was not working and was receiving Social Security Disability and food stamps). My parents had turned down her request for money for a number of reasons. Anna had written them a very critical letter, quoting scripture about fathers not provoking their children to wrath (Ephesians 6:4). My Dad thought it was positive that Anna was quoting scripture, and wrote back to her to ask if he could visit. She agreed, and he went to Springfield, and even attended one of Anna's counseling sessions. Before the session, my Dad had spent about three hours alone with Anna. He had taken extensive notes during their discussion. He wrote to me, but declined to tell me the details of her counseling session to avoid inflicting further pain. He did say that he believed that Anna's "repressed memories" were "utter fabrication." He did not believe I was capable of the things Anna had told him I had done to her.

Ultimately, I did request my Dad's notes. Some things in the notes carried a grain of truth, and other things were simply false. One of the true things was that Anna told my Dad that I allowed myself to be angry and hurt, but that I did not allow Anna this. Anna said I never felt her feelings were important. She told my Dad she used to cry herself to sleep, and cry out to God to take her home. She said she was active in Sunday school and church camp work when we lived in Wyoming. If she misbehaved, I sent her to the pastor. Anna told the pastor she was angry, and the pastor told her anger was a sin. For a long time, she thought that God was always standing there with a big stick with which to hit her when she did something wrong. She stopped going to church, saying that she was taught that she was dirty and useless. There is more. It is unprintable. After reading my Dad's notes, I was deeply sorry that he had been exposed to all that.

In spite of what Anna had told my Dad, they had come to an amicable relationship, and her anger towards him had dissipated. My Dad set up another meeting with Anna for February 14th, but had to cancel that meeting on February 13th. Anna was fine with the cancellation and ended the phone conversation with "I love you, Grandpa." I am so thankful she gave him that last memory of her.

Pastor Gary asked if I wanted my Dad to speak at the funeral. I said I did, if he felt he was able. I also expressed a desire for my nephew, Peter, to speak at the funeral and at the graveside service. Anna and Peter had been "buddies" since their early years. They were only about a year apart in age. Pastor Gary was agreeable and enthusiastic about this.

We were about to finish up our discussion with Pastor Gary, when, with fear and trembling, I asked whether to have an open or closed casket. I wanted it open. I needed to see my daughter again, not just for a moment or two. At the end of our meeting, when I asked Pastor Gary about this, my daughter Beckie spoke up and said, "Well, we have to have it open." I was surprised and very thankful to the Lord for this specific answer to prayer. My son-in-law Gary had helped bring about this change of heart. Nathan did not object. Pastor Gary guided us in the funeral preparations, and we decided we would have the casket open for the visitation on

Tuesday, March 4th, from 6-8 p.m. The casket would be closed for the funeral service, but then open after the service for everyone to see her one last time. Then the family was to go to another room while the casket was closed for the last time. It did not happen like that.

I had asked Nathan and Cheryl that I be allowed to pick out the clothing for Anna. When we arrived in Springfield, that task had already been accomplished, and some things from Anna's apartment had been brought to Nathan's. I was hurt, but found out later that Beckie had picked out the clothes. I thought that was a good thing. I was advised by all the Springfield relatives not to go to Anna's apartment. It was a pit, full of trash, and smelled terrible. I did not go, but later regretted that I had not. Was the Lord protecting me? He did a lot of that during those early days.

We were getting bits and pieces of information from Anna's friend and former partner, Susan. Susan told us about some of Anna's "multiple personalities." There was one named Raymond. Susan said he had "black devil eyes." Anna talked often about Raymond's attempts to "kill" her. Anna spent some time with Susan at Susan's apartment, the night before she died. Around 11:00 p.m., Anna went home to walk her dog. Susan called Anna to ask if she was okay. Anna said she was "safe," which was the term she used to describe Raymond's activity in her life. Later, we found out that the night of February 27, 1997, Anna told Susan that Raymond was trying to kill her with her dog's leash.

About 10:30 p.m. on March 2nd, we went to bed. We stayed with Nathan and Cheryl. We'd stayed with them for the past several years, whenever we went to Springfield. The four of us get along very well, and we thank God for our good relationship. I have wondered what it would be like to go through this kind of tragedy with animosity among the major people involved.

Nights and mornings were awful. At night, all I could do was think. If I gained a few hours of sleep, the reality of it all came crashing into my consciousness in the morning. Anna was dead. It seemed so surrealistic, at times, like it did not happen. Then, reality would set in. It *did* happen. We needed to be up, on Monday March 3rd, at 10:00 a.m. to meet with the funeral director, Paul. Again, we slept fitfully.

CHAPTER FOUR

Day Four—March 3, 1997

FUNERAL ARRANGEMENTS

We had a little breakfast Monday morning, March 3rd, and then headed for the Herman Lohmeyer Funeral Home in Springfield. Nathan drove. We brought the clothes and jewelry for Anna to wear. She was to wear a blue print blouse with a blue cable knit long-sleeved sweater and white slacks. Nathan found earrings in her apartment from a silver dolphin necklace and earring set I had given her. We found a different dolphin necklace to go with the earrings. Anna was wearing some rings that were gifts from her friends. Susan had given her a ring and wanted it to be buried with Anna. We showed the mortician a recent picture of Anna, so he would know how to do her hair.

Anna had recently posed for a series of "Glamour Shots," which Susan had requested and bought. Many of them are wonderful pictures. I was given these, as well as the proof sheet. I had reprints made, and they are displayed in our home. These pictures are of great comfort to me. I had not seen Anna since October 1995. We had a print framed and placed on a "memory table" during the visitation. We were not even sure we would have a memory table—because of how she died—but we never tried to hide that fact that Anna committed suicide.

We decided to display a few other things on the memory table. There were a few items from her dolphin collection, and several other memory-laden pictures of Anna. We also displayed a porcelain baby shoe that had her name, birth date, birth weight and length on it. Susan asked to display a heart-shaped candle that was a gift from her to Anna. We kept it lit during the visitation.

Paul, the funeral director, was very gentle. We saw the room where Anna would be laid out. We gave Paul some music tapes we wanted played during the visitation. I went to the casket room to see the one we had chosen. It was not ostentatious. Anna's nails were quite discolored, and Paul told us they would have to put some nail polish on them. I found out later from the Deputy Medical Examiner that this was the condition of livor mortis. I had trouble taking all this in, but later my nursing education surfaced. Anna had hung in her closet for nearly 15 hours, and all her blood settled in her hands and feet. Her neck was also severely traumatized.

Our half of the funeral cost was $1,714.57. Paul told us we could come after 1:00 p.m. the next day, Tuesday March 4th, to see Anna. We walked around the room where Anna would be laid out, trying to comprehend it all. I was on automatic pilot; pre-programmed to do whatever needed done.

After the four of us left the funeral home, we stopped at the St. Louis Bread Company restaurant and had a light lunch. I did not feel like eating, but I knew I had to keep up my strength. We drove by the cemetery to see the plot, and then drove by Anna's apartment so I could see where it was. I did not ask to go in.

When we arrived back at Nathan's, we were all emotionally spent. The next day would be a busy one. Don, a dear friend from Chicago, had called and left the message that he would be at the funeral. We were surprised, but thankful. He had known Anna well. They used to sing duets in our living room. Don understood her better than I did, maybe because he is also gay.

My immediate family would be arriving the next day. We just spent time around Nathan's house Monday evening. Beckie, Gary and Michael, my grandson, came over. It was the first time I'd seen Michael in almost a year. He was quite shy with me. After a bit, he pointed to me, and asked his mother Beckie, "Is that Anna?" There was a long silence, as everyone recovered from this unexpected question. Beckie said, "No, Michael, that's Grandma." Michael asked, "The white-haired Grandma?" We all laughed, and Beckie said he gets me mixed up with my Mother! He was not too far off, as by this time, I felt as if I had lived a dozen lifetimes.

CHAPTER FIVE

Day Five—March 4, 1997

THE VISITATION

On Tuesday March 4th, we slept in a little. It was a gorgeous, warm, sunny day. The temperature would reach 69 degrees. Susan was coming over, and we wanted to see her. Susan and Nathan spent the entire morning talking. We discovered many details surrounding Anna's death, and of her last few weeks. While Susan and Nathan were talking, they listened to some of Anna's favorite music. I did not participate in their discussion, as I had not been invited, and did not want to be rude.

Bob and I talked with Cheryl about lunch for the day of the funeral. Cheryl decided to visit her father, who was in the hospital with a serious illness. Bob and I went to the grocery store to get lunch items and paper goods. We did not know whether others would bring food, so we planned to buy some Kentucky Fried Chicken right after the funeral. We needed to be prepared. Bob and Nathan washed and cleaned their cars. More mundane tasks.

My sister called to say that they and my folks were at the motel and wondered if we could stop by after we had seen Anna for the first time. We also had a meeting with Pastor Gary set up for 4:00 p.m. so that he could meet my Dad and Peter, both of whom were to take part in the funeral. There needed to be some order to the service and that was to be decided at this meeting.

We finally left for the funeral home about 1:00 p.m. As I was getting ready, all I could think of was that I didn't want to be doing this. Wasn't there some way of escape? *How* could I be going to a funeral home to view my daughter's dead body? This wasn't happening to me.

But—yes, it *was* happening to me. Everything in me rebelled. Where was the "God of all comfort," the one who had "put His arms around me" on the way to Springfield?

When we arrived at the funeral home, someone was already in the room with Anna. I was *so* angry. We were *all* upset. We asked Paul, the funeral director, to tell the person in there with Anna to leave immediately. I could not believe this had happened. How *dare* anyone see our daughter before we, her parents, did? Later, I found out this is common in Springfield. People call the funeral home for visitation hours, and then assume the body will be ready in the early afternoon of that day. Nathan, Cheryl, Bob and I went in to see Anna, after the person left. It was so surreal to look at my daughter, lying in that casket. I had not seen her for a year and four months. She was larger than I had ever seen her. She had gained quite a bit of weight since our last visit, in October 1995. Her hands were two shades darker than her face. She had nail polish on, which she never wore. The nail polish did little to cover up her blue fingertips. There was a lot of makeup on the inside collar of her blouse. We just assumed that her neck was a mess from the dog chain around it for 15 hours. Later, when I viewed the pictures the Deputy Medical Examiner had taken, I saw that was true. We pulled the blouse collar up around her neck, to hide the makeup. We wandered around the room awhile, looking at the flowers that had been sent. We made our way back to the casket to stare in disbelief. Then we wandered around the room again. We were trying to keep in touch with reality, because it was all *so* unbelievable.

The flowers were pretty and comforting. I never knew how meaningful flowers were at a funeral. I thought it was a waste of money. I no longer think that. There were 31 floral arrangements by Wednesday morning, just before the funeral. We chose yellow carnations as the casket piece. The funeral director Paul placed a "Dear Daughter" ribbon on the spray, and Beckie asked for a "Sister" ribbon. Beckie later reminded me that yellow was Anna's favorite color. I had not remembered that when yellow was chosen for the casket spray.

One flower arrangement gave me a problem. A woman Anna was involved with for a short time had sent a bouquet of peach-colored roses. We later found out that their breakup happened the weekend before Anna died, and had devastated Anna. We moved the roses from beside the casket to another place, and moved my brother's family's flowers beside the casket. I wanted the casket to be surrounded by family flowers. I cannot explain that.

We stayed for an hour or so, and then left the visitation room. Beckie wanted to be alone with Gary her husband, when she saw her sister for the first time. We all went back with Beckie, later, to see Anna. Anna really did not look too good. How *good* can a dead body look? Beckie and I touched Anna. She was so cold and hard. Beckie said she felt she needed to cover Anna with a blanket because she was so cold. I understood what she meant. I also knew it would not have helped.

We finally left the funeral home, and stopped by the Comfort Inn where my family was staying. My Mom and Dad, sister and brother-in-law, brother and sister-in-law, and nephew and his wife were all there. It was a painful greeting. We all just stood around. No one knew what to say. I could not cry much then. My tears were (and still are) very unpredictable. We were glad we had that first meeting with my family before that night's visitation. My sister gave us some cinnamon bread. We had forgotten to eat lunch. My sister said I must have gallon jugs full of tears in heaven. Psalm 56:8 says, "Thou tellest my wanderings: put thou my tears into thy bottle: are they not in thy book?".

We went back to Nathan's home for our meeting with Pastor Gary. It was almost 4:00 p.m. The evening's viewing started at 6:00 p.m., and we wanted to be there by 5:30 p.m. Would there be more "early" arrivers? I hoped not. The pastor, my Dad and Peter arrived, and we had a final discussion about the service. Pastor Gary would talk about the particulars of Anna's life—date of birth, schooling, date of death and method. It never occurred to me to hide the fact that she committed suicide. Then Pastor Gary would call Peter and my Dad to say a few words.

Peter wanted to give the Gospel clearly and my Dad was concerned about what to say. He wanted to speak about the struggle—the war—he perceived to be going on inside Anna. He wanted to talk about her battle between good and evil, and her "sin" of homosexual activity versus living for the Lord, but he didn't want to offend any of Anna's friends who would be there. Pastor Gary strongly encouraged my Dad to speak to those issues. I firmly believed this piece of the puzzle should be brought into the open and addressed. A part of me wondered if her lifestyle "choice" contributed to her death. Since she was a Christian, perhaps she could not resolve these conflicts in a satisfactory way. Was the term "gay Christian" an oxymoron? Perhaps Anna could not fight any more. My Dad agreed to pray about how he could gently address this. There were hugs all around, and then Pastor Gary went on his way and the rest of us left for the funeral home.

When we arrived, Bob noticed the peach roses had been moved back next to Anna's casket. My brother's flowers had been moved away. I became very angry with this—so angry that I did not shed one tear the entire evening. At my request, Bob switched the flowers again. We began an intricate, perplexing, painful and difficult three hours. I was thankful that the visitation had been limited to two hours. Most visitations in Chicago are from 3-9 p.m. In St. Louis, I remember the visitations lasted two days!

It was very difficult for me to see so many lesbians attend the visitation. A little voice inside of me said, "Remember, these people matter to God, too!" I did not listen to that still, small voice of God.

Members of the gay community seemed to come in droves, holding hands, looking hard and sad. They stayed and stayed. A couple came who knew Anna when she was a hospice social worker. Anna had met them when their infant grandson had died. The man was in a wheelchair, and someone said he had AIDS. Their love for Anna was very apparent. They placed a tiny, crystal teddy bear in the crook of Anna's arm, and asked that it be buried with her. In the guest registry, they wrote: "Baby Charles, [their grandson] and Anna in heaven together forever."

A middle-aged man stood in front of the casket, weeping, as he placed a single yellow rose on Anna's arm. He said he and Anna went to the same church, Metropolitan Community Church, in Springfield. Gays, lesbians, bisexuals and transgenders (GLBTs) mostly attend MCC. Many of the attendees are evangelical Christians who have been rejected by mainline denominations. This gentleman said Anna had a beautiful voice, and that her singing had deeply touched him.

Susan told us that Anna had sung at Springfield MCC a few weeks before her death. Anna was very musically talented, and wrote many songs and sang them while accompanying herself on the piano. On one Sunday morning, Anna told the MCC congregation that she wanted to "reclaim a song from her past." The song was *For Those Tears I Died,* by Marsha Stevens, an openly gay, Christian recording artist. I was quite familiar with this wonderful, Christian song and had sung it myself. Anna had trouble singing the song that morning, so Susan and the church pastor stood by her side and helped her through it. Anna sang the song a second time, as the congregation stood and joined hands. This time she "belted it out," Susan said, and there was not a "dry eye in the place." We chose Marsha Stevens' recording of the song for the funeral service. The chorus says, "And Jesus said, 'Come to the water, stand by My side. I know you are thirsty, you won't be denied. I felt every tear drop when in darkness you cried, and I strove to remind you that for those tears I died.'"

My cousin Barb came to the funeral from St. Louis. Anna had been on her mind a couple of days before her death. Barb said she felt the Lord urging her to contact Anna. Barb promised Him she would. That never happened. Later, Barb sent us Pam Thum's recording of *Life is Hard, but God is Good.* How true!

One moment that evening stands out in my mind. Nathan and I were standing at the casket and he said, "What we did 29 years ago lies here before us." Nathan had worked very hard to help free Anna from her pain and struggles. Anna either did not want to, or could not be free. What *did* happen that caused Anna to choose suicide?

After everyone else was gone, we left the funeral home about 9:00 p.m. We went to a pancake house for supper. I was not hungry, but again, I ate just to keep going. My Dad bought dinner for all or us. He had a saying, "He who prays pays." He was the first one to ask to say the blessing whenever we went out for dinner! We were very glad to be together. We went to bed late, even though the funeral was the next day. It would come all too soon. It would be a painful time for us.

CHAPTER SIX

Day Six—March 5, 1997

THE FUNERAL

Wednesday, March 5th, was rainy and very cold. The day before had been a sunny 69 degrees. I wanted a day like *that* for the funeral. The four of us ate a light breakfast, then left for the funeral home about 9:00 a.m. The funeral was scheduled for 10:00 a.m.

Don, our dear friend from Chicago, was the first person we saw when we walked into the funeral home. He had to leave right after the funeral. How glad we were to see him! Since then, he has been one of the faithful few, and sent us cards on the 28th of every month that first year of Anna's death. I introduced him to a few others, then wandered around waiting for the service to begin. The casket was in the chapel surrounded by 32 floral arrangements. The clinic where I worked had sent flowers that morning. The clinic's associate director had called the biggest Springfield newspaper to find a funeral notice with the name "Anna." I was impressed. People began to arrive by 9:30 a.m. I waited for Pastor Gary and the pianist. I was edgy.

About 9:45 a.m., Bob and I went into the chapel and sat down. I never did look around much to see who was there. I was pretty well zeroed in on my family members, constantly looking to them for comfort and support.

Nathan went to the main door of the funeral home and greeted people as they came in. He doesn't enjoy sitting and waiting and I thought it was very courageous of him to greet everyone. Cheryl sat next to me. We were Anna's two moms. Oh! How we both hurt! I asked Susan to sit with us, but she sat with our friend Don. She had met Don during a visit to our home with Anna in 1994. I was not aware, until much later, that Susan did not want anything to do with me. She still does not. She felt I was the root cause of all of Anna's problems. Maybe she even blamed me for Anna's death. Maybe she was right.

We had piano music because Anna loved the piano so much. The pianist played many wonderful, familiar hymns, including *How Great Thou Art*, which is one of my favorites. During the service, we played Marsha Stevens' recording of *For Those Tears I Died*. Many of the same people who had attended the visitation came to the funeral. This surprised me. It was comforting to know that so many people cared about Anna.

Pastor Gary began the service by talking about Anna's life. He talked about Anna being with the Lord, also. I regretted that we did not tape the service. I cannot remember much of what was said. Peter, my nephew, spoke next. He gave a clear Gospel message, that Jesus Christ died on the cross for the sins of *all* mankind. All we had to do was receive Christ's forgiveness and put our trust in Him. Peter told the audience that Anna had done this when she was four. He made himself available, in case anyone wanted to contact him. He did a fantastic job. I hoped he would have some peer credibility since he was the age of Anna and many of her friends.

My 85-year-old Dad spoke next. He tactfully, lovingly and gently addressed the deep war and conflict he believed was in Anna's soul. She was a "gay Christian." Her family and churches had told her all her life, that *she* was an oxymoron. She could not be both gay and Christian.

Pastor Gary ended the service with what Anna might say if she could speak to us. I am not clear exactly what he said, just that heaven is a wonderful place and that we should accept the Lord as our Savior. Then we could join her in heaven when we died.

The service ended with a taped version of *Amazing Grace*. The funeral director then said the casket would be open for all those who wished to pay their last respects to Anna. I remained seated with Bob and the rest of my family for all this time. People came and greeted us after going by Anna's casket. My brother wept, and all he said was "Oh! Mary Lou!" My son-in-law's mother said, "You have given the supreme sacrifice. You have given up one of your children." I knew she was right. I later pondered her words. I thought, "That's what God did. He gave His Son—that was the *true*, supreme sacrifice." I often think God understands my pain because His Son died *hanging* from the cross.

We finally got loaded into cars for the drive to the cemetery. Nathan drove us. We had no limousine as they are expensive and apparently most folks in Springfield didn't use them.

When we got to the cemetery, the people from the funeral home directed traffic. A tent and chairs had been set up, so a number of us were able to sit down, and we were given blankets for our laps. It was very cold and windy. I've been to *so* many graveside services like this, but I never "got" to sit down before. That was always reserved for immediate family members. And now I fit into that category. I didn't want to. The pallbearers took Anna from the hearse to the grave opening. These were all young men who were either Anna's friends or relatives. My nephew gave a brief message of hope from I Thessalonians 4:13-17 and prayed. It was over. Or was it just beginning? It was so cold and windy that no one stood around long, which was truly a blessing, as by then, I was pretty much non-functional and had no words left to give others. Truth be told, I wanted to run away from *everyone*, and not talk to another soul for the rest of my life. But, of course, I didn't.

We piled back into cars and headed to Nathan's house where Bob picked up our car and went to KFC to buy some chicken. He was gone nearly an hour, and I was so worried about him. I had visions of him having been killed in a car accident and since we were from out of town, no one would know whom to contact if something had happened. That was just the beginning of many years in which fear would almost take over my life. However, the problem was that KFC had to fry more chicken because they didn't have enough to fill our order. In retrospect, we should have called ahead.

Our families ate lunch at Nathan's home. My family was there and most of Cheryl's family, also. Cheryl's sister took over and helped in the kitchen. People had brought spaghetti, potato casseroles and brownies. Peter and his wife had to leave after lunch to catch a 7:00 p.m. plane in St. Louis—so all of my family decided to go. There was nothing else to do. My mother and sister had brought photo albums with pictures of Anna, but I could not look at them just yet. We wanted to stay an extra day with Beckie, to go through Anna's things at her apartment. That plan was not well received. I think my Springfield family was trying to protect me. We decided to pack and leave for St. Louis about 5:00 p.m. Nathan and Cheryl needed time with her family and it was obvious to me that everyone needed to get back to his or her familiar routines, and "do their own things."

On the way out of town, we got turned around and ended up very close to the cemetery, so we stopped by to see Anna's grave. I don't know why we didn't just plan to do that in the first place, but as I look back, it seemed we were "misdirected" by God! By this time, the sun had come out, but it was still very cold. There was a mound of fresh red dirt, with several floral arrangements on top of the mound. We had asked the funeral home to take the other flowers to a nursing home or hospital. As we stood by the grave and I sobbed and sobbed, Bob prayed. It was so spontaneous and such a comfort to me! I gathered up a few ribbons from the flowers, and the one from our casket piece that said "Dear Daughter" and "Sister" and we headed for St. Louis.

We finally arrived in St. Louis about 9:45 p.m. We had a good visit with my parents, and my sister and her husband. This was when we heard about my Dad's plan to get Anna to His Mansion in the northeast part of the country. It's a place for troubled young people—drugs, alcohol, broken families, etc. Even though Anna was over the age limit, the director had told my Dad that he was sure something could be worked out. It was not to be and likely would not have helped. It might have been something akin to an ex-gay ministry. After having a bite to eat, we finally went to bed around midnight. Again, I slept fitfully. I wanted to go home. I needed to figure out how to rebuild my "nest" without Anna in my life.

We slept in the next morning, then all went out for brunch. My Dad prayed again first and we headed for home and got back to our house at about 4:00 p.m. There were nine messages on our answering machine and lots of cards. But we just unloaded the car and went to New Community, the mid-week service at our church. We needed to be there. We ran into a couple who we knew casually as we were getting our supper there. Lois said to me, "Are you okay?" The look on my face must have betrayed my painful emotions. I told them what had happened and they invited us to sit with them. It was good to be with Christian friends in our church.

The next day, Friday, March 7th, was taken up with lots of odds and ends; unpacking, working out and trying to arrange to get our new furniture delivered—which finally came at 2:30 a.m. Saturday morning, March 8th! There were more phone calls to people who didn't know yet, and more tears. Bob slept in on Saturday morning, as he had gotten to bed at about 3:30 a.m. I got up and went to our church for a *Living in Hope* AIDS awareness seminar. I missed the pastor's message, but caught him on the way out and told him about Anna. He prayed with me then and there. My friend, Linda, was on the panel for the seminar and I wanted to be there to support her. After the seminar was over, I told Pat (the coordinator of the seminar) about Anna. She cried and hugged me and then told Tom, one of the pastors at our church. He came up to me later and offered to help Bob and me in any way he could, so we took him up on it and had three meetings with him. He did a good job of getting us through those first few weeks.

II

THE MIDDLE

CHAPTER SEVEN

INFORMATION FROM NATHAN

On Monday, March 10th, I returned to work. I am a registered nurse and was the coordinator of a free HIV clinic. I was still numb, but did not know it. I stood in my office and sobbed, repeating, "I don't *want* her to be dead. I don't *want* her to be dead." I had been at the HIV clinic only six weeks before Anna's death. I wanted to make sure my boss understood that I didn't expect to be paid for the week I was off, and his comment was, "Well, that's just too bad!" They never docked my pay one penny and gave me two raises after Anna died. A God-thing? You bet!

Over the next two months, I did little more than cope. I went to work every day, but couldn't get down to the basics of housekeeping, like cooking, laundry, and cleaning. Thankfully, Bob understood and did many of those tasks.

About two and a half months after Anna's funeral, something physical happened to me. One night, in the middle of May, I became very short of breath after walking on my treadmill for twenty minutes. My neck and jaw tightened, and I had an irregular heartbeat. As a nurse, I *know* what I would have told anyone else with the same symptoms: "Go the Emergency Room. Now. Do not pass go, do not collect $200!" I didn't do that. I waited until the next afternoon. Since the symptoms persisted, I finally went to the Emergency Room. It was amazing. The staff there didn't let *me* pass go or collect $200! They had me in a cubicle, on a heart monitor, and an IV started all within about 20 minutes. I was having about eight to ten premature ventricular contractions (PVCs) per minute. You are allowed only six. They admitted me to the hospital for treatment and observation. I was started on a heparin IV to keep my blood thin and clot-free. I was put on a beta-blocker to keep my blood pressure low. A cardiologist visited me the next morning, and offered me two options: undergo a heart catheterization (angiogram), or undergo an echocardiogram and an echo stress test. I opted for the latter because I'm chicken! The PVCs went away with exercise, and the echocardiogram was normal. Twenty-eight hours later I was sent home, almost $5,000 poorer! The cardiologist's parting words were: "The good news is your heart's fine. The bad news is we don't know what *is* wrong with you." But

I knew. My daughter was dead. I thought I was coping well, but my body was telling me I wasn't.

Bob and I decided it might be time for me to have some counseling. My boss suggested a man in our town, who is also a member of our church. I had known about this guy some years back, but had forgotten all about him. I knew I needed someone with the same belief system I had. I entered counseling with Steve, and then, the truly *hard* work of grieving began. It continues to this day.

After a few sessions of just information gathering by Steve, the tears began to flow, both in his office and at home. Sometimes I would cry for three or four hours. How was I going to get through this? I didn't know. I didn't think I ever would. I was not even sure I wanted to.

It was during those first weeks of counseling that it became clear to me that I had to get more information about what Anna's life had been like the year and a half or so before her death. What events transpired to lead her to such a desperate act? What emotional pain was she in? And, what happened those two days—February 27th and 28th, 1997? I *had* to know more than what I had been told.

The first thing I did was to call Nathan and Cheryl and ask if they would be willing to come to our home and talk to us about what *they* knew about Anna's recent life. They agreed to do so and came to our home in mid-July 1997. Just before they came, I wrote in my journal: "I'm feeling apprehensive about the visit from Nathan and Cheryl. Bob told me last night while we were at the home of friends, that Nathan told him he doesn't want to tell me about the counseling session he went to with Anna. I have such mixed feelings about wanting to know what was said in that session. I feel like a lot of people know what Anna blamed me for, but *I* don't know. Nathan used to say: 'There's a little bit of truth in everything you say.' So I guess I wonder if there *was* any truth in Anna's so-called repressed memories." Would I really be able to *hear* all that Nathan had to say?

We visited for hours, with Nathan doing most of the talking. I listened and took notes. I kept my emotions under tight control, because I knew if I wanted to gain information from Nathan, I had to show him I was strong enough to take it.

Following is some of what he told me:

- Anna was on Klonopin (a heavy-duty anti-anxiety medication), Reglan (for stomach problems), Pamelor and Paxil (antidepressants).
- Anna smoked marijuana. She ran out of it the night she committed suicide. She claimed marijuana calmed her. To compensate, according to Susan, she took extra Klonopin. (My Nursing Drug Reference book lists "suicidal tendencies" as a side effect of Klonopin.)
- In the past year, Anna never seemed happy. She was unable to sustain relationships and was even severing them. She was drinking heavily.
- Anna may have been schizophrenic. She loved the role of victim. She was sick and gathered people around her who would support her sickness.
- Anna told Nathan her relationship with me was always bad. She was the mother, and I was the child. I leaned on her and put pressure on her. I manipulated her into doing what I wanted. She felt responsible for my life. She cut off our relationship in August 1996, so she could gather strength to build a different relationship.
- Anna said I emotionally and sexually abused her. She said I destroyed her whole life.
- Anna's counselor told her it was okay to hate people and not forgive. That is what she did.
- Nathan attended a counseling session with Anna in which he told the counselor that he feared for Anna's life and that he was just watching Anna spiral downwards.
- Anna thought my major concern was myself, not her. She did everything in her power to avoid conflict and hated herself for not being more confrontational. Anna thought I always got my way, and that she had to surrender.
- Anna said I used guilt as a wide, double-edged sword as a means to control her.
- Anna did not believe there was safety with me. She thought I would "whip" her with whatever she said.
- Anna felt my love was conditional, and that she could never be "good enough."
- Anna carried all her pain around, fed it, and nurtured it. It had become much worse during her last year.
- Anna was unable to get through a day at work. She had to quit and go on disability, or they would have fired her.
- Anna was in group therapy, as well as individual therapy. All that went on in the group therapy was griping and complaining. Nathan said the group therapy was "insidious," allowing their roles as "victims" to pull them together.
- Anna appeared on the Jerry Springer show in October 1996. She was supporting one of her friends from her therapy group. Her friend was on the Springer show to confront her mother. At one point, Anna's friend threw a chair at her mother. This was an Anna I had never seen.
- Anna was trying to integrate 26 personalities. Personality "Raymond" had shown up recently, was evil, and getting stronger all the time.
- Susan believed "Raymond" came out and killed Anna, and Anna doesn't even know she's dead.

Nathan had told Anna that he would talk to me, since things were so bad between us. Anna didn't want this to happen because she thought Nathan would side with me. One of her "little-girl" personalities, "Karen," told him this.

Nathan said that society builds frameworks in which people can be dysfunctional and survive. The social sciences are doing everything to "crash and burn" society, just like the devil. They are not making people take responsibility for their actions.

Nathan told us he believes that sociology today builds frameworks in which people can be dysfunctional and survive. The social sciences are doing everything they can to "crash and burn" society, just like the devil is. They're not making people take responsibility for their actions.

Nathan said we will all rationalize Anna's death, so we can accept it and cope with it. He said I needed to acknowledge my part in her death, learn from it, and move on.

Nathan also revealed Anna's financial status when she died:

• Anna's assets included credit life insurance which would pay off her credit card and she had a pickup truck worth about $3,500. She also had a $20,000 life insurance policy. Susan was the beneficiary. Susan gave Nathan $5,000 for Anna's nephew, Michael. She had $1,200 cash available from an income tax refund and SSDI. Also, Anna had apparently purchased about $100 worth of CD equipment the day before she died. (Does this tell us her suicide was an impulsive act?)
• Anna had many debts, but her creditors—school loans, doctors, credit cards and hospitals—forgave all.

Nathan gave me an audiotape of Anna's songs. She wrote the words and music, and accompanied herself on the tape. (See Appendix A.) She also wrote the following poem a month before she died:

> This body is like a prison
> That binds me to another time
> Reminding me of the torture
> And the scars it left behind
> Every violation touched my very soul
> And though I long SO, but I fear NO
> Will this body ever truly be mine?
> Defective! I feel defective!
> This body screams its ritualistic wounds
> And my soul is shredded into fragments
> Lost within the tomb...of this body.

After hearing all Nathan had to say, I went into the kitchen for something to drink. Nathan followed me and asked, "Are you okay?" That was all it took. I burst into tears. Nathan was very kind, and we talked for an hour. That is, he talked and I listened. He told me I had to figure out who I was and be at peace with that. He also said I needed to rid myself of the guilt I've carried around and learn to forgive myself and understand God's love. Yeah, right! Could this happen? I doubted it!

I felt sad for Nathan. He had tried so hard to get Anna to really *talk* to him. He loved her dearly, and I know it was difficult for him to relay all that information to me.

CHAPTER EIGHT

PHYSICAL EVIDENCE

I still had more questions. Just before the first anniversary of Anna's death, I searched for more knowledge, beginning with a series of letters. I sent letters to the Deputy Medical Examiner who had signed Anna's death certificate. I wrote letters to the police. I wrote to her psychiatrist, and to each of the psychiatric hospitals in which Anna had been a patient. I wrote to Anna's therapist at the time of her death. Many advised me not to write these letters. But I had to. Just because you know the ending of the movie *Titanic*, does not mean you leave halfway through the film. I knew the ending. Anna was dead. I needed to know what occurred during the months we had no contact. I needed a glimpse of what happened in the minutes before she died.

Shortly after I wrote and sent my letters, the details surrounding Anna's death began to come together. The Deputy Medical Examiner, Ron, sent me a copy of the "Death Scene Checklist" I had requested. This is what is known as the Coroner's Report. Ron also sent the photographs he had taken. I was advised by many not to look at the pictures, but these were the last minutes of my daughter's life. I *had* to know what had happened. The pictures were excruciating to look at, but something in me just forced me to stare at them. There were only three of her face, neck and head. The others were of numerous tattoos all over her body. There was a photo of the chair she kicked out from under her. A few photos were of her upper arms, showing self-mutilation marks.

After receiving this report by mail, we decided to make another trip to Springfield to talk with Ron in person. He told us what occurs in a hanging death—answering a *huge* question of mine: Did Anna suffer? It is Ron's belief that she did not.

Ron told us how time of death is determined. There are three criteria used to approximate time of death: 1) liver temperature, in which a small incision is made in the abdomen over the liver and a temperature probe is inserted; 2) the amount of livor mortis—the cutaneous dark spots on the dependent portions of a dead body, due to the gravitational pooling of blood; and, 3) the amount of rigor mortis—the stiffness that occurs in a dead body.

Ron went on to say that, depending on surrounding air temperature, a dead body loses about a degree to a degree and a half of body temperature per hour. When Anna was found, her body temperature was 84.4 degrees. If normal body temperature is 98.6 degrees, that's a difference of 14.4 degrees. The time of death was affixed at 12:30 a.m. Anna's body was not found until 3:30 p.m., an elapsed time of 15 hours. Ron graciously answered our other questions: Why no autopsy or drug toxicology? He said there were none because of the state's Sunshine Law, which says suicide is not a crime. In Illinois, where Bob and I lived at the time, it *is* a crime—that of self-murder. In Illinois, suicide requires an inquest and a coroner's jury to rule on the cause of death. When it's obvious that a suicide has been committed, the state where Anna lived chooses not to spend $950 of the taxpayers' money to perform an autopsy.

Some of Ron's photos showed what he called "self-mutilation" marks. I knew that in the past, Anna had made some rather weak attempts (or so I thought) at suicide. *How could I have been so blind?* In fact, in her senior year of high school, she ingested a whole bottle of 100 aspirin tablets. An hour later she became really frightened and called to me from her bedroom. It was about 1:00 a.m. As soon as she told me what she had done, I immediately took her to the hospital, and she was given activated charcoal to absorb the aspirin and kept overnight. I seems redundant to say that I did not take her suicide attempts seriously enough!

Anna spent two months in a psychiatric hospital beginning ten days after that attempt. It was a grueling two months for us. She was in the hospital over Thanksgiving, Christmas and New Year's. It was a difficult experience for all of us and I handled it poorly.

After our visit with Ron at the Medical Examiner's Office, we went to the Springfield Police Department to meet with the reporting officer. We had read his 23-page police report. The report listed that 43 photographs were taken. I tried to get copies of them, but was informed that all photos had been destroyed. Photos were kept only for 90 days if no legal action was pending. The police officer was unable to give much information that was not in his report. He did say that he thought Anna's body was taken down from the closet bar, before 911 was called, because someone had tried to revive her. He said this is common. Someone tried to save Anna's life. His report showed six witnesses to Anna's demise. The former apartment manager made one of those statements. J.W., the young man who found

Anna, had summoned her. The manager was also Anna's friend. She states,

> *Upon entering Apt. #100... I observed Anna, who resides there, hanging from a dog leash. The print of the chain was in her neck. Her body was blue/cold and she, in my opinion, was already dead. Nevertheless, I took her down and felt for a pulse, attempted to clear her airway. The process took approximately three minutes...*

I called this woman during our visit with the police officer. She added a little to the story. She said Anna had a disagreement with a lady upstairs the evening of February 27th. The statement from the woman upstairs said,

> *Anna called and I was upset with her for prying into my children's family life. Anna had told them if they were disciplined to let her know. I told Anna to stay away. She was close to my children so when she came home, she came to my apartment and tried to "smooth things out." I was upset and asked her to leave. I didn't want to talk to her mad. She asked me to talk to her tomorrow and I said okay. About 30 minutes later, she left a note in my door, knocked, and ran downstairs before I answered. I waited to hear from her today, February 28th, and never heard from her.*

Also during this Springfield trip, I tried to contact the young man, J.W., who had found Anna. But he had moved from the apartment complex, and no one knew where he was.

We went to Anna's apartment complex hoping to see an apartment like the one Anna had. We spoke to the manager, the third since Anna's death. He said, "You know, I heard something about somebody committing suicide here, but I figured it was just a rumor." We said we wished it *had* been just a rumor. He then said to us, "We've been doing some clean-up work here in the complex, and I just evicted some people out of your daughter's apartment. It's vacant. Let's take a walk." We were able to see the very place where Anna had lived and died. It was very tiny, and the only word that comes to mind is "shabby." I finally understood how her suicide took place. It was a garden apartment with high ceilings and the strongest, highest steel clothes-hanging rod I had ever seen in *any* closet. It was painful to think of that chain around her neck. I had been told it was the dog's leather leash. But, a *chain?* Those steel links tearing at the flesh on her neck and face? The pictures told the story. I wonder, was she aware of that pain?

CHAPTER NINE

MENTAL ILLNESS

Susan's statement, from the police report, tells a story of Anna's severe mental illness. In part it reads:

> I have known Anna for the past three years. Throughout this time, Anna has been in continuous individual and group therapies in order to deal with past abuse issues, primarily sexual abuse. In the last three years, Anna has hospitalized herself voluntarily at Cox North Hospital and Research Hospital in Kansas City due to suicidal ideations. Over the past five months, Anna has been through enormous changes, including ending a 2 ½ year relationship with this reporter, changing residences three times and quitting her job [as a social worker] and beginning to receive disability for major depression. Anna has also been in and out of several relationships during this time. She had continued a close relationship with this reporter and often discussed the difficult time she was having managing life on a day-to-day basis. She has spent many nights either at my home or me at her home when she did not feel "safe" enough to stay by herself. She has had intermittent ideations of killing herself by overdose, cutting her wrists, hanging herself or shooting herself. My last conversation with her was February 27, 1997 around 11 p.m. at which time she reported having some thoughts of harming herself, but when asked, she told the writer she was "safe." In the past, she has always been able to state to this reporter honestly when she felt unsafe and we would discuss what she needed to do to keep herself safe. Last night, she told me she was safe, made plans with me to go see old friends this weekend, and turned down an offer for her to stay at my home for the night.

I first became aware of Anna's childhood sexual abuse in September 1994. Anna had called at the end of August that year to let us know that she and Susan were coming to Chicago for a seminar. They would like to stay with us, but Anna said they were used to sleeping in the same bed. If we were uncomfortable with that, then they would gladly stay in a motel. What a quandary! I wanted my daughter in my home, but not under those conditions. I called a friend whose gay son had died of AIDS a few years prior. She suggested that I restate my position—that the Bible calls homosexual activity a sin—but that it was very important to me to have a relationship with Anna, and then allow them to stay at our home and sleep in the same bed. When I told Anna, she was surprised! "Wow, Mom! You've come a long way." I did not think so. I just wanted all of this to go away. However, that was the beginning of a very good period in our relationship.

Prior to Anna and Susan's visit, I had listened to a broadcast on our local Christian radio station on the topic of homosexuality. The man being interviewed was Joe Dallas, then head of a group called "Exodus International," a Christian organization in California geared to helping Christian kids come out of the "gay lifestyle." He said that one hundred percent of the lesbians he counseled were sexually abused as children. This was true of only about fifty percent of the gay men he counseled or so he claimed.

I had also been reading the book, *The Wounded Heart—Hope for Adult Victims of Childhood Sexual Abuse*, by Dr. Dan B. Allender. In the hope of gaining some insight into why Anna had *chosen* the "gay lifestyle."

During Anna's visit in September 1994, I left the book lying around, hoping Anna would ask about it. She did. Angrily, she asked, *"Why* are you reading this book?" I replied honestly that I wanted to gain some insight into the pain in her life. Anna responded by blurting out that Stan Mosher [not his real name] raped her when she was seven. I shrieked, *"Why didn't you tell me?"* Anna told me she was afraid I would not believe her. I *did* believe her. This guy was a distant relative of mine and I knew for a fact that he had committed incest with his own sister when Anna was only about three. Stan was ten years older than Anna, making him about 17, which occurs to me as a time in a young man's life when the hormones are flowing freely. It was definitely plausible.

Permit me to add a caveat there. At the time of her death, Ann was seeing a counselor who apparently told Anna that her problems were due in part to some repressed memories from her past. I am aware that no therapist can confirm the validity of a repressed memory. Nor am I able to do so. To my knowledge, Anna's female counselor was not a Christian and she was definitely not a biblical counselor, evidenced by the report to me that the therapist told Anna that it was okay to hate people and she didn't have to forgive anybody. I suspect the words "people" and "anybody" really meant "mother" to Anna.

Ironically, I remembered that in 1995 I heard a *Focus on the Family* radio broadcast, hosted by Dr. James Dobson, on "False Memory Syndrome." The broadcast's guests were Dr. Paul Meier, Dr. Paul Simpson and David Gatewood. Three statistics were mentioned: 1) Seventy percent of female therapists were victims of abuse as children; 2) Sixty-three percent of clients sue their therapists for implanting false memories; and 3) One in four girls is sexually abused by age 14. Whew! There's more.

Since I made the choice to believe Anna, based on the past history of Stan Mosher, I was devastated and heartbroken for her. Maybe this explained some things. Some of the pieces of the puzzle of Anna's life began to fit together.

That same day in September, Anna told me that her Sunday School teacher in Colorado had also molested her when she was nine years old. When asked why she had not said anything, she said, "Mom, he told me if I told anyone, he'd go after Beckie," Anna's only sibling. After Anna returned to her home from that 1994 visit, she called and thanked me for believing her. I struggled to understand.

I continued reading Dan Allender's book after that visit from Anna. He further states, "The tragedy of abuse is that the enjoyment of one's body becomes the basis of a hatred of one's soul. Abuse arouses within the victim a taste of legitimate pleasure in a context that makes the enjoyment a poison that destroys" (p. 86).

There had been other incidents of molestation when Anna was in her early teens. She told me that a distant, much older, male relative had molested her when she was about 13. Another incident occurred when she was 16, by my male employer at the time. Anna had stayed with his family for a few weeks so she could finish high school in Wyoming, while Bob and I moved to the Chicago area. For some reason, I assumed—and said as much—that these incidents must have been precipitated by Anna. Oh! What a terrible mistake *that* was! Even if it was true to any degree at all, I now know that the adult in the situation is *always* the responsible party, not the child. What I didn't pick up on was that Anna was very troubled and in great emotional pain. She was crying out for nurturing, for love, for comfort, for stability. I gave her almost none of that. Nor did Anna seek comfort from the Lord, and I didn't point her in that direction because I continued to be so self-centered.

Among Anna's personal effects was an undated poem Anna had written that tells a pathetic, insightful story:

> *Shaken, rattled, rolled*
> *Beaten, battered, broken*
> *Are our souls from years of pain and strife*
> *Hurt so deep inside that there seems nowhere to hide*
> *So we fight to keep familiar what is known*
> *And in fighting to protect ourselves*
> *We find that we reject ourselves*

And drive away the ones who'd help us heal
When we find we are alone
And the safety is all gone
For the sand we've let it slip right through our hands
Can we open up a window to our souls?
Can we let in what is needed to be whole?
Can we let go of control?

In his book, *The Wounded Heart*, Dan Allender asks, "Why does abuse make it so hard to come to the Lord for the succor and life that our souls crave? What is the enemy to the healing process?" Allender goes on: "...the answer is shame and contempt. The damage of past abuse sets in motion a complex scheme of self-protective defenses that operate largely outside of our awareness, guiding our interactions with others, determining the spouse we select, the jobs we pursue, the theologies we embrace, and the fabric of our entire lives" (p. 21).

I noticed Anna pulling away from me at the beginning of 1996. She didn't call or write and claimed she did not have a phone where she had recently moved. During her Masters in Social Work program, Anna had been seeing a therapist in the Kansas City area and continued with this woman for some time after she finished her Masters degree and moved to Springfield. Apparently, the hour and a half drive to Kansas City was getting to be too much for Anna, so she started seeing a woman therapist in Springfield. For a short time, she saw both therapists. Anna had been in counseling for as long as I can remember after the suicide attempt during her senior year of high school. When she lived with us, we made certain her counselors were Christians. We had no control over her choice of counselors after she moved out and never met any of them.

Anna's Springfield counselor told her she had "repressed memories," and diagnosed her with multiple personality disorder. Anna was told she had 26 different personalities. Anna's psychiatrist, who prescribed her medications, doubted that diagnosis. He diagnosed Anna with Borderline Personality Disorder, which is characterized by instability in relationships, impulsive behaviors, and wide mood swings. The psychiatrist also said Anna had several other conditions: Atypical Depressive Disorder—mood disturbances that were not altogether characterized by sadness, but again, wide mood swings; Dissociative Disorder—a condition characterized by sudden, temporary alteration in the combined functions of consciousness and identity; and, Post Traumatic Stress Disorder—a state of anxiety precipitated by a traumatic event that involves re-experiencing that event. (All definitions taken from *Mental Health – Psychiatric Nursing* textbook.)

Dan Allender offers this explanation: "The external outworking of the damage done by sexual abuse is evident in two broad forms: 1) secondary symptoms (depression, sexual dysfunction, etc.) and 2) the 'typical' way the abused person relates to others. The style of relating to others is lived out in a daily, discernible form" (p. 144).

Anna's therapist claimed to unlock "repressed memories" in Anna. Did this counselor "unlock" the memory of Anna's rape when she was seven?

Dan Allender alludes to the fact that many people become aware of memories of abuse during the counseling process. He states, "In order to see the potential signs of abuse in the symptoms presented, it is imperative to know what to look for. Significant signs include the symptoms of depression, sexual dysfunction or addiction, compulsive disorders, physical complaints, low self-esteem and particular styles of relating" (p. 145).

A newspaper article on February 16, 1997, in our local paper, was headlined, "Study Says 25% of Adults Can Be Made To Believe False Memories." The article stated, "Given a few bogus details and a little prodding, about a quarter of adults can be convinced they remember childhood adventures that never happened." The article further states, "The experiment is one of a series of exercises psychologists have developed that can plant false memories in the brain. Once they take root, these thoughts often become as real as genuine ones—indeed perhaps even more so. Over time, people may forget things that did happen and remember things that didn't." Scary!

But, in the psychiatrist's progress notes and in hospital records, there were other problems addressed as well—situations that, in my mind, could not be true in any sense of the word. A report from Kansas City's Psychiatric Research Hospital reads, "[Anna] described long standing satanic ritual abuse by her mother." The report further reads, "The patient on admission talked about her mother's sexual perpetration and that she has used tattoos rather than self-mutilation sometimes when the feelings to hurt herself appeared. She talked about ETOH [alcohol] enemas vaginally and rectally and a rape when she was eight years old." This same report also stated that "[Anna] states she has plans to murder her mother." More shock. More pain. More confusion.

Anna was obviously mentally ill. But how much of it was induced by my poor choices and the painfully true statement that I did not love her unconditionally. In his book, *The Road Less Traveled,* M. Scott Peck says of those undergoing psychotherapy "Of the minority who stay in therapy, most [people] must still be taught to assume total responsibility for themselves as a part of their healing. This teaching—'training' might be a more accurate word—is a painstaking affair as the therapist methodically confronts patients with their avoidance of responsibility again and again and again, session after session, month after month, and often year after year. Frequently, like stubborn children, they will kick and scream all the way as they are led to the notion of total responsibility for themselves" (Pp. 295-296).

At one point, after Anna's death, my daughter Beckie said Anna had told her she'd been hypnotized by her therapist to remember repressed memories. An American Medical Association report says that we just don't know if repressed memories are true or false. A social worker friend in Colorado told me about "TCM," Therapist Created Memories! He also told me Multiple Personality Disorder was the "fad disease of the '90s." I do not know if Anna truly suffered from either of these disorders. I only know what the progress notes of her psychiatrist say.

In March 1996, around the time of my birthday, I received a very perfunctory phone call from Anna about 9:45 p.m. She had not sent a card as was her custom, and did not seem to want to talk much. She apologized for not saying much, stating that she was watching a TV movie. I heard nothing more from her for some time after that birthday phone call.

Then in May 1996, I did not get a Mother's Day card from Anna, or even a phone call. I was deeply hurt, and at the end of July, I wrote her a letter. In part, my letter to her said, "My heart is very sad. I don't know what I have done to cause you to be out of touch with me, but I truly would *like* to know so that I can make things right between us and ask you to forgive me." I went on to tell her about one of our cats that was sick and I would be taking her to the vet, knowing that the possibility existed that we might need to have her put to sleep.

On August 4th, 1996, I received a very terse letter from Anna, stating in part, "It is not acceptable to me for you to have [the cat] put to sleep." The type-written letter ended with, "For the moment, this is all I have to say.

Another letter will follow when I am ready to send it. This communication has only to do with the cat." She signed her letter, "Anna," not, "Love, Anna." Her letter started out "Mother," not "Dear Mother." I knew in my heart there was serious trouble. My stomach was in knots. On August 1st, we had our 13-year old kitty put to sleep due to a severe thyroid condition. There was a remote chance the condition could be treated, but the procedure was prohibitively expensive. Anna called on August 2nd. I was scared to death to tell her what we'd done, but I knew I had to. Anna was kind about it and said "It sounds like you did the right thing."

That was the last time I ever heard her voice.

I received a letter from Anna, on August 12th, 1996, in which she severed all ties with me and blamed me for all her problems in life. The letter was single-spaced, typewritten, and a page and a half in length. I quote most of it for you below as this is the last communication I had from Anna—ever:

August 8, 1996

Mother,

I began this letter on June 3, 1996, and it is time for me to finish it.
This will be the last communication I will initiate with you unless I think I can, or want to, handle something else. I would appreciate it if you would respect that. I do not want to talk to you on the phone or receive letters.
The reason I am writing is to finally respond to the last card and letter I received from you. I realize that Mother's Day must have been sad for you. I choose not to take any responsibility for that. I have been taking care of myself, and I have been remembering things that happened to me as a child, both at your hands and mouth and at the hands of others. I believe that inside you, you know what I am talking about. I choose not to give you details about my memories because I believe you would only try to use them against me. Suffice it to say that I feel enraged about the childhood you and others have stolen from me. I have been left with broken pieces like shattered glass. But I am beginning to put them together as I heal. I know the truth within me. Your statements on the phone of "Even if it's not true," and "I hope I remember the same things you do" only strengthen my belief in myself and my truth. They would not have been necessary if you didn't know inside what you and your family have done to me. It felt to me that you were making those statements in an attempt to make me doubt myself. I won't. I can't. You stole much from me as a child. I choose to take it back and live my own life.

It is my opinion that your tears for Mother's Day were only for you and what you didn't get. I have been crying tears and screaming rage for years. Only now, I know why. I believe you know as well or you would not have sent me the Employee Assistance Program brochure. This program, by the way, only works for employee *children if they are 25 years old or younger, and then only if they are still in school. I did check it out in the hopes of getting some financial relief for my therapy. Currently, I spend approximately $350 a month on therapy and medications to help me through this. My insurance does not cover it unless I am seeing one of their providers. I am already established with therapists I trust, so I am carrying the cost.*

As in your card, your letter was not about me. It was, again, about you; what you want and need in order to feel okay about yourself. I cannot, and will not, attempt to make you feel okay. I sacrificed me to do that for too long. If you want to really feel okay about you, seek the counseling you need and truly work at it. You have every right to feel however you feel about this letter; but you have no right to hold me responsible for your feelings. That is no longer my job. It never should have been. Your issues are yours and mine are mine. I am dealing with mine the best way I know how. I am becoming an individual, separate from you. No matter how much it hurts inside, and how painful the memories are, you cannot fix the colossal damage that has been done to my soul. Nor do I want you to. I do not trust your words because they are not followed by trustworthy actions. Not only that, your words can be painful and shaming. I don't need that. As I said before, I gave my life and individuality to you from the time I was born. I no longer belong to you. I belong to me. I do not care what you believe, think you know, or deny. I no longer need you to be my mother. You never really were a true mother; other than the fact that you gave birth to me. I don't want you in my life now. I may never. No matter how much you ask, I cannot, do not want to, and do not have to, forgive you. Your own actions have driven your children away. I do not plan to come back because I do not believe that you will choose to truly change. That takes a tremendous amount of work on your part.

I know that reading this is probably making you angry and sad, as you deny or realize what you have done. You cannot hurt me anymore. Your pain is your own. I am writing this letter for me...to break the tie. If you need or want to talk to someone about this, call a therapist. I have no desire to listen, and I don't want you calling my sister or my father about it. This has nothing to do with them. This has to do with you and me. If you try to contact me, your letters will be returned unopened. I will not talk with you on the phone. If there is a major emergency, you have my pager number: Remember to enter your number and the # sign after the computer voice and the beeps. If it is not an emergency and I call, I will not stay on the line.

I need the space to heal. Right now, I cannot fully heal with you in my life. Heal thyself, mother: I am home. Please leave me alone.

Truly, Anna

I guess it's pointless to say that I was devastated by the letter. I cried for hours. I sought counsel from friends and family and it was universally recommended that I abide by Anna's wishes. Later, though, I wished that I would have at least sent her a birthday card on October 22nd of that year.

Maybe Anna was testing me to see if I really did still love her. Her test was to push me away—completely. I did continue to write cards, buy gifts, put cash (instead of checks) in her cards, and save them all for a time when things might be better between us. I continued to pray daily and fervently for Anna as I had always done, but struggled because this letter seemed to literally come out of the blue. At the time, I had no idea what I'd done to precipitate this and prayed fervently that if I *had* done something to Anna during her childhood, that the Lord would help me remember it so I could confess it and make it right. No *specific* memories came to mind but I knew in the deep recesses of my heart that the divorce had much to do with her pain, and I was beginning to understand my "child-neglect."

Later that fall, Nathan told me that Anna had been admitted to Kansas City's Psychiatric Research Hospital on the recommendation of her counselor. We were later informed that the purpose of this was to provide documentation that Anna was unfit to work, needed to quit her very good Social Work position in the rehabilitation department of a local hospital, and go on Social Security Disability—all of which Anna did. And Anna knew the ropes. She knew what to say to get herself admitted to this hospital, and to cause them to declare her unfit for work, due to mental illness. The "Initial Diagnostic Impressions" given at this hospital were Major Depressive Episode, Severe Post-Traumatic Stress Disorder, Multiple Personality Disorder, Rule Out Dissociative Disorder, Rule Out Intermittent Explosive Disorder, Rule Out Marijuana Abuse, Rule Out Borderline Personality Disorder, and Worsening of Suicidal Ideation with Plan. With all of these diagnoses why they discharged Anna after one week is beyond me, but undoubtedly not beyond the requirements of the insurance company. Anna's financial problems were evident after she quit her job.

At one point during all of this research on my part, Beckie told me about "Rachel," another one of Anna's personalities. The psychiatrist mentioned "Rachel" in his notes, describing her as the one who "flies into rages." Apparently Rachel wanted Anna to be in pain so Anna had gotten many tattoos on her back and other places, supposedly to satisfy Rachel. In the psychiatrist's notes regarding Anna's own belief that she had Multiple Personality Disorder, he states, "I am concerned that she first heard about these personalities only one and a half years ago. It is of interest that she does not describe blackouts and so, many people would say these were not actually separate personalities but names for mood states. If she refuses to integrate these different states but uses them as excuses for inappropriate behaviors, this will only worsen her maturation."

CHAPTER TEN

THE REVELATION

Push the pause button here for a moment. I've already stated that I neglected Anna, did not nurture her, allowed TV, neighbors, friends and school teachers to be her "child sitters." What causes a person to "declare" they are gay? More specifically, what motivated Anna to do this? In November of 1988, Anna went into a treatment center in Parsons, Kansas, reportedly for people with co-dependency issues. (This institution has since gone bankrupt.) She asked me to come to the center and participate in a group session. She made her request at the same time Bob and I were planning to return to Colorado to celebrate our tenth wedding anniversary. I told Anna that I was very sorry, but I could not accommodate her due to the plans for our anniversary. I told her the expense of getting to where she was, in addition to the money we'd already put out to fly to Colorado, and the fact that I had no more vacation time that year made it impossible for us to comply with her request. Another rejection? Yes. Nathan did go, and later told me that I had made a wise decision not to go. He said he was seated in the center of a circle of people/patients at this treatment center and was "systematically annihilated" by the group. It was awful for his wife who had been asked to sit outside the circle and just observe. It was during Anna's stay at this place that she wrote the following letter to me. In some ways, it sums up all the tragedy in her life.

December 4, 1988

Dear Mom,

I guess I should've been honest with you while we were on the phone a week ago. No—no guess about it—I should've said how I really felt instead of saying it was all okay. I feel like I've been saying that all my life. I understand about your job and the house payment and commitments. I really do. But understanding doesn't take away the feelings. I have to own and feel them; they're not going to go away if I stuff them.

I feel really hurt and angry that those things seem to be more important than I am. But I felt afraid to tell you that. When I try to express just my feelings, I feel like you get defensive and must come up with all kinds of reasons why my feelings are wrong. Just because I understand that you can't come doesn't mean I don't hurt about it. I've felt hurt and alone for a very long time.

I feel like you think that all of this is my problem, and if I would just get fixed, everything would be all right. I know a lot of it is my fault; I see my behaviors, etc. But I didn't get this way on my own. Mom, you told me tonight that you always held a special place for me in your heart and you always loved me, but I have not felt that from you. I feel like I have tried to be your perfect child all my life. I feel like you are more afraid of how I make you look, than just letting me be a person. I felt so very alone while growing up. I felt like I was the parent a lot of times. You say that my feelings are okay, but you don't just let me have them and feel them. If I tell you I feel a certain way, you tell me I took your action wrong or I shouldn't feel that way. Even last Christmas in the car when I told you I felt like you didn't listen to my feelings or that my feelings aren't okay, you said, "That's not true." That totally discounted how I felt. True or not, those were my feelings.

I felt like I got two messages from you a lot of the time: "Come here—go away." Even when we talked a week ago, you said how much you love me and want to help, but other things are more important right now. This is not a guilt trip. I just feel confused.

I feel angry that you think I'm not working here [at the treatment center] or that I'll "do it again" [attempt suicide]. That's not fair and you have no right to judge. I know I was manipulative in the past. I see that I used this to get attention and that I just worked the system last time [in the psych hospital]. That's my stuff! But why should I have to be suicidal to get attention? Beckie got most of the attention as a child because she acted out. I was good, and maybe you bragged to others about me, but rarely did I hear it. But when I did stuff wrong, I felt like I was the lowest thing on earth. Mom, hardly ever did you give me specifics on what I had done wrong. Once, during a family session at the hospital, the psychologist and I asked you to say how you felt using "I feel" statements and I remember once you said, "I'm gonna tell you how I feel. You make me sick. You turn my stomach. All you ever do is take and take from this family and you never give anything in return. You're selfish and self-centered, and you never think of anyone but yourself." That last part was standard. I feel so angry with that! I tried so hard to prove I wasn't selfish! I feel so hurt that you wouldn't tell me your true feelings. Your feelings!

Mom, I don't hate you. I felt so abandoned by you and Daddy. I felt like my needs didn't count—like it wasn't okay for me to miss him so much or talk about him after he left. I felt like if I told you how much I was hurt, it would only hurt you more—and then maybe you'd go away, too.
But I needed you to love me, and comfort my hurt. I know you couldn't. I was so afraid and lonely, I thought if I did everything right, things would be okay. But I felt so guilty when I couldn't fix things. I felt caught in the middle of you and Beckie and sometimes of you and Dad.

I'm afraid to tell you my feelings or be assertive with my identity because I'm afraid I'll lose you forever. I already feel so far away from you. I feel you withdraw from me emotionally when I say things you don't like or can't handle. Like last year when you told me to move my stuff from my bedroom to the laundry room when Grandma and Grandpa came for a visit. When I asserted myself to ask why and said I didn't feel I bothered them, you dropped the whole subject like a hot potato, saying "Fine. Do whatever you want. I don't care." It was like you shut big iron doors and totally shut me out. You did that a lot, and I felt so rejected and abandoned.

I also felt so hurt when you didn't believe me about Dr. Mike. I need you to want to protect me and hold me, but you blamed me and I felt so angry and rejected!

Mom, I know all the reasons for the divorce from Daddy's point of view. But I only have his side of it. That's not fair. I want yours, too. I know these things aren't one-sided. I want to give you a chance to tell me how you felt during all that.

There are some things you need to know about me, that I need to own up to. I know I manipulated and controlled, or tried to control you at times to get what I wanted. I used Daddy to referee our fights and that wasn't fair. I wasn't honest with my feelings and I hid a lot from you, things like smoking and drinking, or where I was going. I didn't give you much opportunity to know me for me, because I played so many games and had so many faces. But this is over now. I am being honest, and I need to lay who I am on the table. I need for you to know—I don't know how to say it and I'm scared.

Mom, a lot of things have happened in my life with regard to my sexuality. Men have taken advantage of me, and I always thought I was wrong to have sexual feelings at all. I've fought so hard, so long to understand and be comfortable. But now I am. I'm comfortable with women, I love women. I don't want to be with men. I want to be gay.

Maybe this will be the last straw. This is me, Mom. Who I am, what I feel and have felt. Who I plan to be. I still hurt so much about some things, but I'm working on those.

Mom, I love you. I really do love you. I can't change you. I don't want to. I need for you to know how I feel and who I am. What you decide to do with it is up to you. I'm letting go. Please don't try to change me or anything. All I want is for you to love me. If we can have a real, honest relationship, I want that, too. I do need you. No matter what, you're my mom. But I need me to do what I need to do for me. I don't need you or your approval to make me happy or okay. I strongly desire your love. I don't want to hurt you anymore. I know I have with my anger; my suicide attempts, and lots of things. I love myself just the way I am. I'm changing and growing every day. I love God, I know He loves me. I'm letting go of the anger and pain, slowly.

Mom, I truly love you. Please believe that. I've always loved you. I always will. .Respond if you wish,

I love you,
Anna

I became physically ill and sick to my stomach, after reading Anna's letter. Was it because of what Anna revealed about being a lesbian? Maybe. Was it that I knew she was right about the way I had treated her for the last many years, but couldn't bear to admit it to myself or her or anyone else? Where *was* I? Why didn't I really *hear* her? I did respond to her letter with my own. In part, I wrote the following:

> *Undoubtedly, the most difficult part of the letter was the gay thing. I will* never *accept that in you. I feel it's a terrible waste, besides being spiritually and morally wrong. For a reason that I don't quite fathom, I have a harder time dealing with that issue than almost anything in the world. Did you know that about me? I do, and will continue to love* you, *but I will always hate that, and will pray every day that you will change your mind and attitude. You see, I have never believed, nor will I ever believe that anyone is* born *with that propensity.*

> *Regarding the other things in your letter, I'm glad you were able to honestly share with me—but I don't feel anything would be gained by answering your letter point by point. I don't see it all the way you do, nor do I remember treating you the way you feel I did as you were growing up. Needless to say, I've hurt you very deeply and in very many ways. I recognized this 3 years ago, and I think, at that time, I asked you to forgive me. I can only hope that someday you will be able to do that.*

> *I am willing to answer any questions you would like to ask about the divorce. I did not volunteer any information to you as you were growing up, not wanting to burden you with that. But, I will try to answer your questions if that would help. My feeling, though, is that more would be accomplished if we could do it face to face. I will say this much, I have a great deal of respect for your Dad, especially in the last month or so. He has helped me a lot and I feel that he is the best father you and Beckie could ever have. I love and adore Bob and always will, but over the years, I have matured some, I hope. I have had to face the fact that had I been more mature (much more) eleven years ago, that your Dad and I would still be together. I am willing to accept much of the blame, though not all. As I look back, I think one of my major problems was not being in touch with my own feelings, and therefore, unable to communicate them to your Dad. I deeply regret all this, but I cannot change the past.*

These letters, at times, make me feel like I murdered my daughter. Where *was* I when Anna was in so much pain? Recently, I heard a message at church titled, "God's Heart Toward the Homosexual." One sentence that the pastor said just *screamed* at me. He said, "Look in the mirror before you look out the window." That sentence pierced my heart!

Two months after Anna's death, I heard a letter read on our Christian radio station. I wrote and asked for a copy of the letter. It was just the beginning of a change in my attitude and thinking about the homosexual community. Oh! How I wish I'd understood this before Anna died. The author of the letter, Kerry S. Doyal, Pastor of Lake Region Bible Church, in Illinois, answered my request and included a cover letter with some context and explanation:

April 28, 1997

Dear Friend,

I am honored that you have requested a copy of my letter. It is a joy to make it available to you. I give you permission to copy it and pass it along to others. Feel free to personalize it for your own use with homosexuals you may know and love. Maybe submit it to your local paper. Ours ran it unedited! I care little about receiving credit. I am excited to see God use it any way He sees fit!

Allow me to give you a little context. The letter you have requested is the one I read at an Open Forum at College of Lake County, Illinois (a local two-year college) sponsored by the Spectrum Club, a Gay, Lesbian and Bisexual group. They had invited the community to come hear their ideas and ask questions about homosexuality in the '90s.

The previous two Sundays, I had preached on the authority and audacity of Jesus to forgive sinners, even if it meant dealing with the self-righteous wrath of religious leaders (Matthew 9:1-13). As I saw the invitation in our local paper to come to this Open Forum, I wondered if Jesus would go to such a gathering. From my meditation of Matthew 9, I knew that if He went, He would lovingly call people to follow Him, as He did Matthew. This call would mean abandoning an old way of life, adopting His way of life as His disciple, and advocating His life to other "sinners" as Matthew had done. As I wondered if I should go, I thought if anything, I should write a letter of apology on behalf of Christians for our self-righteous attitudes, expressions of condemnation, often minus messages of love. I reasoned that this letter could also be sent to the paper, which carried the announcement on a front page.

I decided to read the letter in church as part of my sermon. It was met with strong acceptance. I then presented it to my elders who helped me clear up a few minor areas. They gave their full blessing to share this with others, send it to the paper, and read it to the Spectrum Club if I so chose. One elder offered to go with me if I decided to go. Undecided about going, I called and asked the Spectrum Club if I, as a local pastor, could come and read a letter of apology and clarification. I was warmly invited to come and read whatever I had.

Taking along two elders, both widely known and respected in the community, I went with great joy to share my letter with all those present. I could not have imagined a better reception. As I read, I could see looks of shock as they heard my words of apology. At least two panel members openly cried. As I finished, the room burst into applause, lead by members of the panel. I presented copies of my letter to each panel member, greeting them as I did. During and after the meeting, several people asked for copies of my letter. I was sought out and thanked by many people who had boldly identified themselves as homosexuals. More than one asked about our church, and said they may come visit sometime! One lady could not believe a religious leader would say what I had. It had been churches' responses that had caused her to quit going to church, she said. Along with copies of my letter, I was able to give out a pamphlet I had written about forgiveness that also featured information about our church. Before going, I had recruited many people to pray for three areas. I asked them to pray that I would have boldness and brokenness and that they would be open. God did exceedingly abundantly beyond what we thought or asked! The next morning, a Christian lobbyist from Springfield, Illinois called, thanking me for speaking up. He asked me to fax copies of my letter to him and some state and national leaders. He hoped to use it himself, as Illinois is currently considering a gay rights bill.

I rejoice that God's timing is so sweet and that He can forgive and even use people like me! I am reminded that it wasn't offended sinners who sought Christ's death, but smug "churched people" who pursued this "friend of sinners" all the way to the cross. Sinners received Him gladly because He received them gladly as well. He provided His love, forgiveness and life transformation. He can and will make forgiven followers out of anyone! He has that authority, the audacity and that ambition.

Finally, if possible or appropriate, let us know how God uses this letter. Our church would love to rejoice with you in each victory, no matter how seemingly small.

A forgiven follower,

Rev. Kerry S. Doyal

The letter I had heard on the radio and which was read at the Spectrum Club is as follows:

April 16, 1997

Dear Friends,

As a pastor of a local church and as an individual Christian, we need to ask your forgiveness. We have carried out offenses against you as individuals and as a community. We have wronged you in many ways and we need to make things right. We have also seen and caused a sad closing down of communication between you and ourselves as individuals and a community.

First of all, often when we have made clear our disapproval of a homosexual lifestyle, we have at times withheld our love and acceptance of you as individuals whom Christ loves dearly. We have been guilty of rejecting you as friends, family, neighbors, co-workers and fellow humans. Such rejection of you, intended or unintended by us, is unacceptable and understandably appalling! We ask your forgiveness.

Secondly, we need to ask your forgiveness for our self-righteous attitudes. We have been blindly self-righteous in focusing on this sin, while conveniently minimizing or ignoring other sins, most especially our own. God is displeased with our sin, too. We have come to see and believe such self-righteous hypocrisy must grieve God's heart as well as wound yours. We need to be equally vexed about our own issues, which are far more pervasive and influential than those of many other groups with which we differ.

Obviously from what I have written, our apology does not mean we agree with or condone homosexuality. We believe from a reasonable, simple study of scripture that homosexuality is one of many sins that offend a holy God. As we would never ask you to approve of sins towards God and others in our lives, we cannot do the same in yours.

[If you are gay, don't stop reading here—please!]

We also ask that you not confuse our disapproval with fear or homophobia. As a family, we have had friends and guests who are homosexuals. They have shared our table, held our infants and enriched our lives as friends. We were honored to have a friend live with us who was HIV positive. We do not disagree because homosexuals scare us. Nor are we afraid that our own sexuality will be challenged, or that our personal sense of masculinity or femininity will be threatened or undermined. Very simply put, we disapprove of homosexual activities (not homosexuals as persons) because we see from the Bible that God does too, as He does with many other behaviors and attitudes. True acceptance of a person without approval of all they do is similar to a parent's unquestionable love for an erring child.

Our great concern about this issue may at times come across as fear. And yes, frankly, some Christians do fear homosexuals themselves. My fear is that homosexuality has, as many other sins do, negative consequences for our nation and community. While such talk may seem hopelessly intolerant, we would ask the freedom and privilege of holding to our perspective—offensive though it may be. To not grant such freedom to us would be itself an expression of intolerance. We grant your probable desire to change our position. We ask the permission in civil discussion and even polite debate to seek to alter your views as well, something we have felt that is increasingly unacceptable in our culture today. It seems a reverse form of fear and discrimination (heterophobia?)

So, while we differ, we agree to be civil towards one another. We will seek to display greater expressions of love, friendship and common courtesy. Just as we understand not all homosexuals are Dahmers, pedophiles, or militant ACT-UP members, so too we ask you to not assume all Christians are hate-filled, gay-bashing homophobics. Neither assumption is true or conducive to better relationships. Sadly, for those "Christians" who are hateful and fearful, we sincerely apologize. We are as embarrassed by them as you may be rightfully irritated. So, while there are gaps we cannot close, there are some bridges we can and must build. We only hope to consistently give you enough cause to allow us to try.

With love from a pretty vile forgiven sinner,

Rev. Kerry S. Doyal
Lake Region Bible Church

Once again, if you're gay, *please* don't stop reading here. Push on. I promise you, you'll be glad you did.

Even though I had read books about the "roots of lesbianism," God seemed to be asking only one thing of me: to love Anna (and all other people, gay or non-gay) as He does. There is no doubt in my mind, that had I had the benefit of these two letters from Kerry Doyal, my whole attitude towards Anna would have been different. In fact, my whole attitude towards homosexuals in general is totally unlike it was before reading these letters. And God graciously allowed me to manifest this new attitude every day, because of my job as the Coordinator of a free HIV Clinic. About 30% of the patients are gay and I was drawn to them like a magnet. Maybe my desire was to do for them, and be towards them, what I never was towards Anna. But my journey doesn't stop here. In fact the road gets more hilly, and the grade is so steep at times that I think I will lose my footing altogether, flip over on my back and fall headfirst into a bottomless, black abyss.

III

THE
BEGINNING

CHAPTER ELEVEN

A VERY SPECIAL JOURNEY

Over the past few years, I have become acutely aware of God's amazing graze. I am astounded by it every day. I want so much for every square inch of my heart and soul to become tenderized by it. God is patiently waiting for me to trust Him *fully* as He has, and is, and always will be trustworthy. It takes courage to trust, and I'm a coward. Maybe trusting does not come easily for you, either. We are not alone.

After Anna died, I began to read voraciously about grief, about grace, about suicide, about almost anything that had the slightest chance of reducing my pain. One of the books I read was Philip Yancey's *What's So Amazing About Grace?* Chapter 13 is all about Yancey's good friend, Mel White. Mel was married and had two children. He had struggled with his sexual orientation since the age of seven, and for the next twenty-five years. He and his wife finally divorced. Mel and his partner, Gary Nixon, have been together more than 25 years. Mel was a ghostwriter for Billy Graham, Jerry Falwell, Pat Robertson and others. He has written several books and produced Christian films. He was a pastor and a professor (at Fuller Theological Seminary) for over 14 years.

In Chapter 13 of Yancey's book, there was another familiar name—Tony Campolo. Yancey states, "I also talked with Tony Campolo, a high-profile Christian speaker who opposes homosexual practice, while at the same time admitting the homosexual orientation is ingrained and almost impossible to change. He holds up an ideal of sexual celibacy. Partly because of his wife's ministry to the gay community, Tony has been slandered by other Christians, resulting in many canceled speaking engagements, as well as having his books returned to the publisher at times. At one convention, protesters distributed purported correspondence between Tony and gay leaders at Queer Nation, a letter that was proved spurious, part of a smear campaign." *(What's So Amazing About Grace? p.168)*

In the Spring of 1999, my dear friend, listener, sympathizer and empathizer, who had lost her twin brother to AIDS, loaned me a book. It was titled, *Stranger At the Gate: To Be Gay and Christian in America, by Dr. Mel White whom I had read about in Yancey's book. Many people wrote commendations of the book:*

> *Mel White gave voice to the Christian right. Then he committed the sin of admission.*—Washington Post

> *Mel White is perhaps the finest writer I know... a man of integrity and fairness.*—Jerry Falwell

> *Finally, we have a book that beautifully reveals the spiritual struggle, the terrible pains, and the legitimate hopes of the Christian homosexual person. I urge every American Christian to read it.*—Lewis B. Smedes

My friend told me the book would be a "fast, easy read" and I'd be able to get through it quickly. I began to read. By the time I finished reading the Foreword by Lyla White, Mel's ex-wife, I closed the book. I knew in a heartbeat that this book was going to take some serious time, prayerful thought, and not a little highlighting in yellow on my part. After all, it had been recommended by Lewis Smedes, a man I knew to be godly and evangelical, and who had spoken at our church on two occasions.

In the Foreword, Lyla White writes, "...after all those decades of trying [to make our marriage work], we discovered that no one can choose or change his or her sexual orientation. Reading this story will help you better understand the homosexuals in your own life. And understanding them—seeing the face of Christ in their faces—will enrich your life and bring you closer to God and to each other." Lyla adds, "We are all on this journey together, and we must ensure that the road is safe for everyone, including our homosexual brothers and sisters who for far too long have been unfairly condemned and rejected. Isn't it past time that we opened our hearts and our arms to welcome them home instead of seeing them as strangers still waiting at the gate?" (p. 7)

This book has had a more powerful and profound impact on me than almost any book I've read in my life. Why? Because I never understood the *struggle* that Anna must have experienced. I never took the time to read or research anything about homosexuality. I had been taught all my life that homosexuality was a sin. Period. The end. No ifs, ands or buts. But now, I was reading a "but..." After some searching on the Internet, I found an email address for Mel White and I sent him a letter thanking him for writing the book, for his honesty and compassion. I told him Anna's story. He emailed me back with a note of deep compassion, grief and understanding.

Mel then told me about a meeting that was to take place in Lynchburg, Virginia, October 22-24, 1999. He called it Soulforce. Mel and his partner Gary co-founded the organization, basing it on principles of non-violence as taught by Jesus Christ as well as two others who looked to God for guidance—Martin Luther King, Jr., and Ghandi. The purpose of the Lynchburg meeting was to get Jerry Falwell to tone-down his anti-gay rhetoric, homophobia, and gay bashing. Such fear-filled speech leads to hate crimes and violence toward gays in this country.

There were to be two hundred of Mel's Soulforce supporters (clergy and laity—gay and non-gay) and two hundred of Falwell's supporters gathering together in the spirit of love, instead of violence. Mel and Falwell had agreed to put their differences aside for this one weekend. Mel invited me to come and tell my story—that of being unkind and saying hurtful things to Anna in response to her letter telling me she was gay. I declined stating lack of money for the trip as my reason.

In truth, I didn't want to go, because I couldn't figure out how to tell the story—that of not loving Anna unconditionally because she was a lesbian.

In the meantime, Bob and I had been praying for a way to go to Charlotte, North Carolina on that same weekend. We wanted to be with my parents, who were celebrating their 64th wedding anniversary. On Sunday night, September 13th, at 10:00 p.m., Mel White called us again. He asked Bob to get on the line, as well. He said he just had to make "one more try."
Would I come to Lynchburg and tell my story if he paid all the expenses? We were very surprised, to say the least. I asked Mel if I could be honest with him. I'll never forget his reply. A man I had never met called me by name and issued an order. He said, "Mary Lou, you must always be honest with me." I replied, "Mel, I have two problems: 1) I do not believe the Bible condones homosexual activity, and 2) I do not want to be known as a 'gay activist'." To my first comment, he said, "All the more reason you need to be there because you can bridge the gap between Falwell and his people and our Soulforce group." To my second statement, he said, "Well, fame has its price." What did *that* mean? I was still skeptical.

What were these "training sessions" Mel talked about? Who would I really be speaking to and for how long? I queried Mel in several e-mails, to relieve my doubts. Finally he e-mailed me back, and I quote: "Your questions show real lack of trust in me. I thought I've been open and very clear from the beginning. But if you continue in this spirit of fear and distrust, anxious to be sure your position is clear about homosexuality, I'm wondering how clear you can be about your position on loving each other in spite of our differences. Jerry and I have agreed that for this meeting, it's time to set aside our differences and come together to speak with a united voice against the rhetoric that leads to intolerance. I'm not sure you're ready to take that stand. Are you?" While his e-mail hurt, I knew he was "right on." *If* God wanted us to go to Lynchburg, I needed to trust Him to bring that about. If he didn't want us to go, I had to trust Him for that, too. Trust?? The opposite of fear?? My life was full of fear since Anna's death. I did not know how to trust again.

And so, we agreed to pray about this and to actively seek godly counsel. We promised to let Mel know our decision. We decided to talk with four people: my counselor, Steve; a woman from our church who was leading a ministry for those struggling with sexual identity; John, our mid-week teaching pastor; and Philip Yancey. From each one of these four persons, we received a clear and positive response: "Go, tell your story. Maybe it will save just one life." John said, "Why *wouldn't* you go?" I responded, "*Fear!!!*" That night, John's message was called "A Bold Heart." It was the story of David and Goliath. I told John I needed a bold heart. Philip Yancey faxed me a full-page letter, saying he knew Mel quite well, and that I could trust him, but ultimately threw the ball back into my court as to whether to go or not.

The bottom line for me was this: We did not believe the Bible condones homosexual activity (yes, we know and have looked up all the scriptures relating to this). ***If you're gay, please don't stop reading here, either!*** Neither did we believe the Bible condones fornication, adultery, pride, greed, murder, lying, stealing, or gossip. We do believe that the evangelical Christian community has elevated the sin of homosexual activity, as opposed to homosexuality per se, above all other sins. We also became acutely aware of the fact that gay Christians are not welcome in the "mainstream" denominational churches. Therefore, they've started their own (quite evangelical) churches—UFMCC—Universal Fellowship of Metropolitan Community Churches. As I mentioned earlier, this is where Anna went to church, and sang *For Those Tears I Died* about two weeks before she died.

We knew attending the Lynchburg meeting might make us unpopular with some family members and friends (if they found out—which they could have, as there were many people from the media in attendance at this forum). We knew we just had to leave that in God's hands.

CHAPTER TWELVE

LYNCHBURG

We decided to go. We flew into Charlotte, North Carolina on Thursday, October 21, 1999, and were able to spend some quality time with my Mom and Dad before leaving for Lynchburg, Virginia about noon on October 22nd. This would have been Anna's 32nd birthday.

We had reserved a rental car and the rental agency shuttle picked us up at the airport and drove us to the lot and the specific location of our rental. It was candy-apple, fire engine, metallic *red*. I knew that would never work. So, I told the lady driving the shuttle what we were doing and where we were going. We had been informed that this meeting in Lynchburg would be picketed by gay activists, *as well* as people who claimed to be evangelical Christians. We wanted our presence there to be understated. Arriving in a bright red car would not be an understatement. The dear lady who was driving the rental car van found us a white car within about 10 minutes (during which time, I had prayed fervently that God would provide a neutral-colored car).

The plan was for me to speak Friday night to Mel's 200 delegates at "Soulforce Central" which was First Christian Church in Lynchburg. There were to be other meetings and training sessions in non-violent response on Saturday. Then I was to speak to Jerry Falwell and his 200 delegates (along with Mel's 200 Soulforce delegates) late Saturday afternoon at a light buffet dinner that was to be held at Thomas Road Baptist Church (Jerry Falwell's church). After that, there was to be a press conference.

When we arrived in Lynchburg we went to the First Christian Church where we registered, received our name badges and packets of information. There were snacks available and many friendly people. There were also uniformed police officers. I didn't "get it," and we felt out of place.

We then proceeded to the Courtyard Marriott where Mel was to have made reservations for us. There was no reservation in our name. But they had plenty of rooms and gave us one right away. As we were transporting our luggage in the direction of the elevator, we saw Mel White and Gary Nixon leaving the hotel. We'd never met. We approached them, introduced ourselves and hugged them both. We went up to our room and tried to relax a bit before changing from our travel clothes into something more suitable for speaking and meeting many new people.

My wonderful brother and sister-in-law had given some very sage advice about what I should wear. They told me to wear the same thing each time I spoke, so it would be easier for people to recognize me. That was good advice. Speaking for Soulforce at Lynchburg was such a new experience for me. I never would have thought about what I should wear.

We returned to the First Christian Church about 6:30 p.m. Everyone began to assemble in the sanctuary as worship music was being played by very talented artists. Mel opened the meeting at about 7:00 p.m. He thanked everyone, and restated the reason we were there. Our purpose was to ask Jerry Falwell to tone down his anti-gay rhetoric that leads to violence and hate crimes. Mel introduced many people who spoke briefly. We were welcomed by Diana Westbrook, who organized the weekend; the pastor of First Christian Church, who said he was honored that we had chosen his church to be Soulfource Central; and even the Mayor of Lynchburg.

There were many that spoke, telling their stories:

A lovely lady named CJ, and her ex-husband Ken, came to the front of the auditorium. They were clear about the relationship they were now experiencing after many years of frustration, guilt and pain. CJ embraced her former husband, and it was obvious she loved him dearly.

Brian, an alumnus of Falwell's Liberty University, recounted his struggle with homosexual orientation while a student at the college. He stated he never dared say he was gay, and we thought it courageous of him to speak about it now while on Falwell's "turf."

A Jewish gay man named Gary spoke. There were about four Jewish men that were part of the Soulforce delegation. They had received a special dispensation to participate that Friday evening.

Jimmy Creech, a heterosexual United Methodist minister, spoke. I found him to be a very special and delightful man. He spoke of "spiritual violence," and stated in the delegate booklet:

> *I believe that the greatest injury done to lesbian and gay persons is caused by spiritual violence. Spiritual violence is the assault upon the integrity and dignity of a person when that person is told that because of who she or he is, she or he is not loved and accepted by God, and is in fact rejected and condemned by God. Damning and judgmental words cause massive and deep wounds that are hard to heal. I believe the spiritual violence must stop.*

Eventually, Jimmy Creech was defrocked and lost his position at his church for officiating a same-gender commitment ceremony. Many Soulforce delegates gathered in Grand Island, Nebraska to non-violently support him at his "trial" by the United Methodist Conference in November 1999.

Then three people, Norman Brown, and Carolyn and Elizabeth Glover told the following story:

> We, Norman Brown and Carolyn Glover, are both teachers by profession and are actively involved in our local community— working on a number of fronts to counter intolerance and celebrate all kinds of diversity. We are also teachers of "tolerance" with our students. Norman is a teacher of children with multiple disabilities, and Carolyn's daughter, Elizabeth, is a student in his classroom. We think that the presence of three loving, gentle, close friends—a white, heterosexual woman, her 10-year-old daughter who has multiple disabilities and is non-verbal (but communicates on a "soul level"), and a black homosexual man who is the beloved teacher of that little girl—will send a strong message that may contradict many prejudices at once.

Lee Ellis, a lovely, talented musician, sang a song he had written. The title? What else?! *Stranger At The Gate*. A word in the song, "Anawim" is the plural form of an Old Testament Hebrew word variously translated as "poor," "afflicted," "humble," or "meek." It is the Anawim, "the lost and forgotten ones," whom Jesus refers to in the Beatitudes in the Sermon on the Mount. "Blessed are the poor in spirit for theirs is the kingdom of Heaven," and "Blessed are the meek, for they shall inherit the earth" (Matthew 5: 3,5). Following are the words to Ellis' song:

Stranger At The Gate
Music and lyrics by Lee Ellis

I was a Stranger at the Gate and you
left me standing there
I was a thirsty man and you had
water but you would not share
I was a laborer by trade, for through
me the world was made
Do you know who I am?
Do you know who I am?

I came a knockin' upon your door but
you would not answer me
I was a child at your table whom
you would not feed
I was a teacher in my time—the living
rhythm the perfect rhyme
Do you know who I am?
Do you know who I am?

Anawim...I am the lost and the forgotten
Anawim...I am the poor and misbegotten
I am the leper and the lame
The righteous and the shamed
Do you know who I am?
Do you know who I am?

When I come knocking upon your
door will you let me in this time?
When I come seeking you out will
you let me find you?
Will you let me show you the perfect way

for the kingdom is here today.
Do you know who I am?

Do you know who I am?

Anawim...I am the lost and the forgotten

Anawim...I am the only first begotten
I am the souls you cast aside
I am the toll at the end of the ride
Do you know who I am?
Do you know who I am?

I am the Lord of all you see
I am in you, you are in me
Can you see who I am?
Can you love who I am?
Do you know who I am?

I am the Stranger at the Gate

Dr. Rodney Powell, a most amazing man, spoke next. He had marched
with Dr. Martin Luther King, Jr. and had participated in the lunch-counter
sit-ins in the '60s. He is also gay. He talked with great knowledge and
experience about the principles of non-violence he had learned first-

hand from Dr. King. We have since become fast friends with Rod and his partner, Bob. They've been together for 28 years and are second only to the love my husband Bob and I have for each other (in my opinion!).

This Friday night service at First Christian Church was to last from 7:00 p.m. to 8:30 p.m. By this time it was after 9:00 p.m. I began to think that I probably would not be called upon to tell my story, much to my disappointment. Then I prayed, and asked God to help me trust Him in all of this. Then I was okay. And a few minutes later, Mel then called on me to share my story. He introduced me as someone "who doesn't really know *what* she believes about homosexuality." To Bob's initial chagrin, he was called upon by Mel to come to the front of the church with me. He did. I had notes on cards so I could refer to them to tell the sad chain of events that led to Anna's death, but there was nowhere to put them, no podium, platform, or even a music stand. Mel stood on one side of me, arm around me, and held the microphone. Bob stood on the other side of me with his arm around me, also. Mel reached over and put his arm on Bob's shoulder. Then, I told my story. You already know most of it. But I want you to get a picture in your mind of what it was like to stand in front of 200 gay people of faith, and tell my story for the first time. Here's what I said:

> *I used to think that the only way to relate to gays was to confront them. I had no use for them. I didn't understand them, and I was judgmental and arrogant. And then that lifestyle touched our home.*

> *Eleven years ago at about 5:15 p.m. on December 8, 1988, I had just walked into the house from work with the mail in my hand. There was a letter from my daughter, Anna. I opened it with the pleasure of anticipation that a mom feels when she hears from her daughter who is away at college. Her letter was dated December 4, 1988. She told me that lots had happened in her life with regard to her sexuality. She said men had taken advantage of her and she always thought it was wrong to have sexual feelings at all. She said she'd fought long and hard to be comfortable and now she was. She said she was comfortable with women. She loved women. She wanted to be gay.*

> *She went on to say she loved me and hoped I wouldn't try to change her or anything. She said that she loved God and knew He loved her.*

> *About two weeks later, I answered Anna's letter. It was December 20, 1988. I told her that I was devastated by her letter. Please allow me to quote this one paragraph from my letter to Anna: "Undoubtedly the most difficult part of your letter was the gay thing. I will never accept that in you. I feel it's a terrible waste, besides being spiritually and morally wrong. For a reason I don't quite fathom, I have a*

harder time dealing with that issue than almost anything in the world. I do, and will continue to love you, but I will always hate that, and will pray every day that you will change your mind and attitude."

Almost two years later, August 13, 1989, I was taking Anna back to the airport to go back to college after she had played the piano at her cousin's wedding. I told her that if she ever decided she wanted to get her act together, she was welcome to come home to live. Unconditional love? No.

What followed were more than seven years of stormy, intermittent encounters. We had a few good times, but not many.

In July 1996, I wrote Anna another letter, because I'd not received a birthday card or a Mother's Day card and had had very little contact with her during that year. I told her I wanted to make things right with her, if she was willing, even though I wasn't sure exactly what I'd done to cause her to pull away from me.

About two weeks later, in mid-August 1996, I received a letter back from Anna. She basically said she wanted nothing more to do with me, that I was her mother biologically only, that I had stolen her childhood from her, and that I had done colossal damage to her soul with my shaming words. She was done with me, and didn't want me in her life, not then, maybe not ever. She told me she could not, did not want to, and did not have to forgive me.

She told me she'd return my letters unopened. She refused to give me her home phone number, and I could have her pager number for emergency use only. And, if I paged her and she discovered it was not an emergency, she would hang up on me. She said she needed space to heal and asked me to leave her alone. I was crushed. I cried for hours.

I sought advice from a counselor Anna had seen when she was living at home, several friends and many family members. To a person, all said the same thing: You must respect Anna's wishes and give her the space she needs. That's what I did.

What would I do now? I would grab my toothbrush, credit card and car keys, drive the 550 miles to where she was living and tell her that I love her no matter what. I didn't do that. Now I never can. February 28, 1997 at 10:00 p.m., I received a phone call from my ex-husband and Anna's Dad. At about 4:00 p.m. that afternoon, Anna had been found hanging from the bar in her closet. She had been dead for 15 hours. It was ruled a suicide by the coroner—no autopsy, no note, no nothing—but days, weeks, months and years of pain and anguish.

I have heard it said that when a loved one dies of suicide, there is a sense of utter failure. And the worst part of it was that I was a failure as a Mom to Anna. I did not love her adequately or unconditionally.

And that's why I'm here tonight. If I can steer one of you away from the pain and anguish I've been living, then maybe Anna's death will have meaning.

In I Corinthians 13, Jesus said, among other things, "Love is patient...and kind. Love is not easily angered, it keeps no record of wrongs...It always protects, always hopes, always perseveres." I displayed none of that.

Throughout these past 2 ½ years, I've had to do a lot of soul searching to figure out just what part I played in Anna's death. I've had to wrestle with who I am and how I treated my own flesh and blood. I've had to repeatedly ask myself two questions and I'm going to ask them again tonight. The first one is: Have I ever been changed by someone's criticism? And the second is: Who are the people who have influenced me by their unconditional love?

The Lynchburg newspaper reported my story in its Saturday morning edition. The article ended with these two sentences: "There wasn't a dry eye in the sanctuary as White hugged Wallner and her husband Bob and asked God to 'take away the guilt. Let it be gone forever.'"

At the conclusion of my brief story, a memorial service was held for all the victims of hate crimes in this country in 1999. About 20 of these people were gay. Delegates carrying poster-sized pictures of each victim walked up and down the aisles of the sanctuary. Included were the victims of the Columbine High School shooting, including Rachel Scott and Cassie Bernall—both dedicated Christians. Ironically, we used to live in Littleton, Colorado, and had we stayed there, Anna would have gone to Columbine High.

There were pictures of the students killed at Wedgewood Baptist Church in Ft. Worth, Texas, and a picture of Matthew Shepard, the gay Wyoming student who had been tied to a fence-post and bludgeoned to death. There was a picture of James Byrd, Jr., the African-American from Texas who had been dragged to his death behind a pick-up truck.

During the memorial service, two of the Soulforce delegates stood up front and read the name of each victim and how they died. No words were spared to soften *how* each person died. It was a candlelight vigil and one so pregnant with sadness and emotion that it's difficult to put on paper.

The meeting was over at 10 o'clock that night. I was unprepared for the amazing experience that followed. People from the meeting formed a line in order to speak with me! So many young people said, "You just told my story. I just haven't gotten as far as the suicide part *yet*." That word, yet, made my blood run cold—three letters that could end a person's life.

A young man named Matt asked me to e-mail him my story. He said several times during the weekend that he wished his dad and I could meet.

Another man, Mark, also asked for a written copy of my story. He and his partner, Lee, were hoping to be accepted as members of their church and were working on that with the Colorado Episcopal Diocese.

Xavier told a lengthy story of rejection by his family. He said often, when his parents came to town to visit his brother and sister, they did not even bother to call him.

Ellen said she had contributed most of the artwork Soulforce used.

Dotti said she wasn't trying to change us, and it didn't matter what we believed about homosexuality. She said she'd been rejected by many of her immediate family. (More about Dotti later).

Gary thanked me for my courage, as did all the people mentioned. There were many others who spoke to me that night. The recurring theme in their comments was, "Thank you for telling your story. Maybe some lives will be saved as a result."

As we left the sanctuary, Dr. Rodney Powell came running up to us, with tears streaming down his face. He thanked us, and spoke of marching with Dr. Martin Luther King, Jr. Rodney was gay at the time, in the '60s, when *no one* was "out of the closet," (at least not anyone *I* knew). He spoke of his partner of many, many years and related a heart-wrenching story. Upon finding out that her son was gay, his partner's mother told him she wished he had died in childbirth. I couldn't hold back the tears.

It was about midnight when we finally ate in our hotel room. After about five hours of sleep, we were back at the church, where we were served a continental breakfast. There were protestors outside the church, carrying signs that said, "God hates fags," "Matt burn in hell," and "Judas Falwell," and other vulgar slogans. We had been instructed by Mel to have *nothing* to do with the picketers. We were not to even make eye contact with them, make any gestures, or engage them in conversation in any way, shape or form. That was difficult, but we did it. We were most grateful for the many Lynchburg police officers who protected us during the entire weekend. I thought, "I finally *get it*." I realized, later, that I did not *get it* at all!

There was no violence in Lynchburg that weekend, just some very misguided people: Fred Phelps, W. N. Otwell (both are Baptist ministers) and Bob Kunst, a far right Gay Activist. To be honest, at that time, I was also a very misguided person—in a different way.

That Saturday morning, it was good to reconnect with the friends we had made the night before. We had never been in the same room with so many gay people of faith. These people spoke to my heart on a deeper level than almost everyone else I knew. I again spoke to many about my story. Paul, a 32-year-old gay man, had sat on a task force advising President Clinton about the gay community. Paul said he advises gays whose families reject them to *keep trying* with their families; to reconnect with them every-so-often and express love to them.

When I started towards Lee Ellis so I could buy his CD with the song, *Stranger At The Gate,* he was walking towards me at the same time, with his partner Mark. They *gave* me the CD, saying they would not let me pay for it. It was then that I asked Lee about the red AIDS ribbon on his vest. He told me the startling news that he is HIV positive. When he heard that I was an HIV nurse, there was cause for an even deeper bond.

The morning activities progressed, including a talk by a "Quaker Buddhist" (I'm not sure what that means, but she was wonderful). Another woman gave us tips on defending ourselves if physically attacked that weekend. The central theme of her message was that we should never do anything that could be construed as a "counter-attack." We were only to protect our physical selves, and not strike back in any way. This must be what it means when it says in the Bible that we are to turn the other cheek.

We were given many "mementos" or "souvenirs" that various people had contributed. Everyone received a Soulforce pin—with the Ghandi/King logo. We received tee shirts with the same logo, as well as a quote from Rabbi Abraham Heschel: "Speech has power...words do not fade. What starts as a word ends in a deed." We also were given buttons with a Jerry Falwell quote: "Is it true? Is it loving? Does it need to be said?" Oh!! If only those three questions could stand out in the front of my mind whenever I open my mouth to speak!!! To this day, I need to continually remind myself of those three questions.

All during the day on Saturday, mention was made of a press conference that was to take place at 5:30 p.m. I finally decided to ask Gary Nixon if I'd be involved in it. Gary said, "Absolutely you will be at the press conference, in fact, Mel said to me last night, 'I think we should just let Mary Lou do the press conference by herself.'" I assumed (wrongly) that there would be many involved in this meeting with the press. There were to be just six of us—Falwell and two of his supporters, and Mel and two of his supporters. I was honored to be one of those supporters, or was I a "supporter" yet?

After our Saturday training session, we were served a delicious lunch by the members of the First Christian Church—cold cuts, potato salad, and a fresh baked pie on every table! Each table was given a fresh pink carnation in a vase to adorn the center. Nothing was too much trouble for these congregants of the First Christian Church. I long to be a part of a church like that.

Before we left to return to our hotels, Sandra, a lesbian from Hawaii, gave each of us a hand-woven Tea-Lei, and kissed us on both cheeks. The plan was that we were to give our Tea-Leis to a member of Falwell's delegation later that afternoon.

Bob and I arrived at Falwell's church, Thomas Road Baptist Church, at about 3:30 p.m. In the small parking lot there were many large vans with TV crews: ABC, NBC, CNN, and others. There was also a group of picketers carrying the same signs we had seen that morning.

Over the entrance door to the activity center, were the large words, "ANTI-VIOLENCE FORUM." The room was filled with round tables seating eight persons each. On every table were eight bottles of water and eight plastic cups of ice. Period. We were supposed to have a light buffet dinner—200 Soulforce delegates and 200 of Falwell's delegates. We never saw a morsel of food. It wasn't until the following Monday that we learned the reason, printed in the *USA Today* newspaper. One paragraph from an article titled "TENSION AND SNUBS, SOME CONCILIATION AS FALWELL, GAYS MEET" reads as follows:

> *Falwell invited 200 evangelical Christians to share tables on Saturday with an equal number from an interdenominational gay rights group called Soulforce. But Falwell's supporters declined to eat with the gays because of what a spokesperson said were concerns that the Bible prohibits dining with sinners.*

There was literally smoke coming out of my ears when I read that! If that were true, no one would eat, and the population of this earth would become extinct! We learned later that some of Falwell's financial supporters had called and threatened to withdraw their support if Falwell dined with us.

Since we were early to the meeting, there were few people in the room.

We noticed a lady sitting at a table alone. I approached and introduced myself to her. She said, "Oh, I read your story in the paper this morning." She got up out of her chair, threw her arms around my neck, hugged me, started to cry and whispered in my ear, "My daughter is a lesbian." She said she was a member of Falwell's church, but would never even *think* of telling him about her daughter. I gave her my Tea-Lei.

Jerry Falwell spoke first. He apologized for not loving gay people and for making derogatory statements about them. But without exception, every time there was a microphone in his face and he spoke an apology, he coupled it with what he believes the bible says about homosexuality. I wanted to say to him, "Jerry, give it a rest! You've made your point. What is the need to keep repeating it?" Spiritual violence? You bet!!!

Mel spoke next. I was so impressed with his response to Falwell. We never heard one unkind or unloving word about Jerry Falwell from Mel White's lips. Again, his request was not that Falwell and his delegation *agree* with him and us about what the Bible says about homosexuality, but that Falwell simply love these people as Jesus does.

After these introductory comments, Mel walked around the room, microphone in hand, and asked some of us to share our stories. Brian, the Liberty University alumnus, said he had always been afraid to talk about his sexual orientation as a student there, for fear of being kicked out. Jimmy Creech, the United Methodist minister, also spoke. Then Mel brought the microphone to me. He introduced me as member of Willow Creek Community Church in Illinois, and again, as someone "who doesn't even know *what* she believes about homosexuality." My talk had gone very well the night before—I hadn't forgotten anything I wanted to say. But that was sort of a "dress rehearsal" and the old adage proved true: If you do well at the dress rehearsal, you'll probably screw up at the performance! And I did. I totally forgot to quote the scripture verses in I Corinthians 13. I was so concerned about the time, because Mel had told me that we needed to leave the Activity Center at 5:15 p.m. to walk to the sanctuary, in a different building, for the press conference. Falwell had taken much more time than he had been allotted, according to the schedule. But then, it was his church, and he could well do as he pleased—and he did.

After a brief rendition of my story, Falwell stood up and pointed to me in the audience. He loudly said, ***"And I hope that mother can forgive herself. She is not to blame, and lacked the kind of counsel she needed."***

My feelings at the moment were: He doesn't "get it" at all.

Of note here is that after my story was told, Falwell said several times what he would do if one of his kids were gay—he would love them unconditionally while praying that they would change.

The Dean of Liberty University then spoke and made the University's position clear. I knew Brian was right to fear he would have been expelled from the University if he had made his homosexuality known while he was a student there.

Then, it was time for the six of us to leave the room and head over to the press conference. Falwell and I ended up walking side by side. I felt honored that I was able to have a brief conversation with this powerful man. I say "brief conversation" because after only a sentence or two to each other, we both fell into a troubled silence. What more was there to be said? On that short walk, we were flanked by plain-clothed police officers. I wish I'd thought to ask Falwell how many sermons on the sin of gluttony he had preached. I'm not proud of that thought. It was judgmental and wrong. Who did I think I was to judge this man? *Who did I think I was to judge Anna?*

At the press conference Falwell's two supporters were the Dean of Liberty University, and a man named Michael Johnston, who had AIDS and had recently come out of the homosexual "lifestyle" as a result of participating in an "ex-gay" ministry that purportedly changes homosexual orientation to heterosexual orientation. Mel's two supporters were Jimmy Creech and myself. This time, I had just two minutes to tell my story. Mel asked me to concentrate on what can happen when parents do not love their children unconditionally. For the third time he introduced me as someone who "doesn't know what she believes about homosexuality." After we each spoke the meeting was thrown open to questions from the large audience of reporters. Nearly all of the questions were directed to Mel or Falwell.

Mel quietly asked if I had anything else I wanted to say. At first I said no. But finally, I felt I needed to briefly address the way Mel had introduced me, so I quietly tapped Mel on the leg and said that I *did* have one more thing to say. This is what I said: "I was amazed and appalled at the number of young people who came up to me last night after hearing my story, and told me that I had just told *their* story. They just hadn't gone the suicide route yet. And, whereas I do not believe the Bible condones homosexual activity, I am acutely aware that I need to look in the mirror before I look out the window."

On the walk back to the activity room where all 400 delegates had watched the press conference on closed circuit TV, I remember thinking that I may have just alienated 200 people by my last comment at the press conference. Yikes!! These dear gay friends had heard me say not once, but three times, that I do not condone homosexual activity. In my mind, they had cause to reject Bob and me altogether. But when Bob and I arrived back in the Activity Center, many, many people continued to come up to us and talk to us, both from the Soulforce delegation and from Falwell's delegation. One Soulforce delegate said to me, "I can't believe you had the courage to share your story *three* times this weekend." Another "God-sighting" in my mind.

Gary, one of the Soulforce Jewish delegates, gave me his Tea-Lei before we left Thomas Road Baptist Church. He didn't think I should leave without one. I was honored to receive it, and tacked it on my office bulletin board for several years.

At the close of this "Anti-Violence Forum," Mel asked all Soulforce delegates to return to the First Christian Church for a light meal. We were all hungry, having expected to eat with Falwell's people. That meeting meal lasted awhile—it turned into sort of a debriefing session. Mel had conceded much to Falwell during the weekend, but he was not willing to concede one remaining matter. It had been agreed that Falwell would preach Sunday and invite all Soulforce delegates to his church. But Falwell had asked Michael Johnston, the "ex-gay" man with AIDS, to preach. Mel told explained that the Soulforce supporters came to hear Falwell preach, not Johnston. A compromise was reached with a cell phone call between Mel and Falwell. Michael Johnston would preach the first service, and Falwell the second. Mel was gracious. However, many Soulforce delegates doubted whether Falwell would keep his word on this matter, and an intense debate started. Mel convinced us that we needed to trust Falwell on this. Finally, Gary Nixon, Mel's lifelong partner, took the microphone away from Mel and said, "Say goodnight, Mel. These people need to eat and sleep!" What a precious man Gary is—quietly doing so much intense and necessary work behind the scenes.

Earlier we had been invited by Dotti and her girlfriend at the time, Angie, to join them and Peggy Campolo (Tony Campolo's wife) and her friend, Kathy, for dinner. We found a lovely and delicious Italian restaurant and had a good meal and time of fellowship. That evening, we ate about 10:00

p.m.— two hours *earlier* than the night before! We exchanged e-mail addresses with Dotti. Little did we know at that time, what a powerful impact Dotti would have on our lives. We finally went back to the hotel to sleep a few hours before leaving the next morning to drive back to Charlotte to be with my folks for Sunday dinner. So, we were not witness to the Sunday morning church services at Thomas Road Baptist Church and had to be content to read about them in *USA Today, Time* magazine and *US News and World Report*.

Our lives were forever changed by that Lynchburg weekend. We came to know and dearly love *many* gay people of faith. I connected on a deep and meaningful level with so many of the Soulforce delegates. Every time I even *think* about what gay Christians have suffered at the hands and mouths of evangelical Christians, I start to cry. And I cry even harder when I think of what Anna suffered as a result of the untruth I'd been taught by my church. This untruth was ultimately the reason I treated Anna as I did.

I wanted to *know* why we evangelicals had elevated the "sin" of homosexuality above all other sins. One possible explanation came from my counselor who said that if preachers could speak against homosexuality (and not so much about other things such as fornication, adultery, gluttony, gossip, slander, pride, and so on), then they would not have to look at themselves so clearly. Makes sense to me.

Once we arrived back in our home town of Elgin, my story was printed unedited in several editions of *The Daily Herald*, with my picture on the front page.

At the time, I had the strong sense that the story that was printed was not the end, but the beginning. I had no idea where God would take this, but I was open and willing to be used in whatever way He saw fit. In a devotional book given to me by Bob's daughter, Lisa, I read these words: "Our blinders are slowing giving way, readying us for the truths we couldn't absorb before." What *was* the truth that I was not ready for? Could it be that God loves and accepts gay people (including gay Christians) just the way He loves everyone else in this world?

CHAPTER THIRTEEN

FRIENDS

Even though I have read many books since Anna died, I had not read anything solely about homosexuality until I read *Stranger At The Gate.* I needed to know more. On a regular basis, a friend at church began supplying me with literature about, and written by gay Christians. Was it possible that God was leading *me* "out of the closet" of my despair and denial. Was *He* giving me a passion for gay people, especially gay Christians? I had never had a *cause* before. Did I have one now? One thing was certain: I had more energy, love and compassion for gay people than I had ever thought possible.

The following stories are about some special friends. Each one has had a unique and powerful impact on my life.

Don

Don had been married for eight and a half years. We had been good friends with both him and his wife. They were Christians, and Don had worked for years at Wheaton College, an evangelical Christian college in Wheaton, IL. And then, on Sunday, November 12, 1989, Don and his wife called us and asked us to come over.

Don's wife wanted a divorce. We weren't totally clear what all had happened, but agreed to simply continue to be their friends, listen, help out whenever we could and to pray for them. I'll never forget the day, less than a week later that they sat in our living room and discussed with us the division of their property. Then we left the room, and they sat at the dining room table hashing it out, item by item. We were somewhat confused and very sad. We didn't know all the details, and just wished we could help them stay together. After all, both Bob and I had been through divorce—and to put it mildly, it is not fun.

They were divorced on January 5, 1990. We were astonished at how very quickly their divorce was final. And finally, Don told us why: he was gay. Did he choose this? I think not. From November 1989 to August 1990, he would come over to our home every Thursday night, have dinner with us and then attend a Christian support group in our town to try to help him "come out of the lifestyle." He later told us that all this support group seemed to function more as a place for Christian gays to get hooked up together, than as a supportive way out of homosexuality. He finally left the group because of disillusionment. In November 1991, he came to the conclusion that he was homosexually oriented and began to struggle with what that meant. In the Fall of 1993, he decided to pursue his sexuality, no matter the theological implications.

Over the years, we chose to love him and be his friend, although we did not agree with his "chosen lifestyle." We talked on the phone and got together regularly. He didn't talk much about his homosexuality. We mostly stuck to "safe" topics—jobs and families. When Anna died, we became very close. He walked each step of our grief journey with us.

Dotti

Dotti is a very "out" lesbian and a committed Christian. She is the one who told us in Lynchburg that it was okay for us to believe anything we wanted to. I wasn't quite sure how to "read" her. Did she really mean that we could believe however we chose, or did she have some "hidden agenda?"

It did not take long to figure out that she was okay with what we believed, but she wanted us to know *her* as an openly gay Christian. And we did learn to know her, and as the song says, "To know her is to love her." Whatever Dotti said to us, we *had* to listen, because she was making so much sense. And she really did not *say* a lot. She just asked *lots* of questions which really made us think.

Just a few days after we arrived home from the Lynchburg weekend, Dotti sent us the following e-mail:

> *Hi Mary Lou and Bob!*
>
> *A quick note—my computer has been down this week, so I couldn't e-mail! But now it is OK! It was such a pleasure to meet both of you! I am sorry for the circumstances that brought you to be a part of our group, but I am happy that you are there! Your presence and story present a powerful testimony that none of us in our society are free until we are all free. Justice for self means nothing if my brothers and sisters are imprisoned in any way. We must make things fair for all! When we realize and accept that our strength lies in our diversity, we can truly appreciate what a wonderful mosaic God has woven!*
>
> *If I had to describe my family motto growing up, it would be "You will tell the truth at all costs." So the first Soulforce Vow—"To seek the truth, to live by the truth and to confront untruth wherever I find it" has been a working philosophy for most of*

my 46 years, but particularly for the last 20 years since I came out of the closet. My family was big on telling the truth until "the truth" was something they did not want to hear.

As an openly gay Christian, my faith in God sustains me—my daily walk with God empowers me in ways I never dreamed possible. I truly don't feel I have ever "lost" anything because of being openly gay. Yes, by the world's standards, I may have lost plenty. But in reality, I have gained more than I could ever imagine by allowing God to work through me and touch my soul in ways that enable me to accomplish things I could never do in my own strength. If I had gained something of value through deception (of who I am), then, to me, that would have simply been a form of idolatry. The truth is, the world was more than willing to give me anything of value I wanted—IF and I say IF I was willing to be deceptive. My faith has allowed me to live my life honestly, however, and to stay committed to accepting nothing, absolutely nothing, if I have to lie to get it.

*I hope that as you continue on your journey, you will consider reading some books such as **What The Bible Really Says About Homosexuality** by Daniel Helminiak as well as **Holy Homosexual** by Michael Piazza (if you haven't already read them). You can go to my website www.empoweringdiversity.com and click onto the "reference" icon and go to the section of books under the "Gay Christian" part to find them and order them. There are many other books also offered there relevant to the topic of "Gay Christian." **From Wounded Hearts** by Roberta Kreider is also good!*

Love and Christ's energy from me to you both! —Dotti

Ah ha!! There it finally was. She was trying to change us. But because I knew *Dotti*, I had to pay attention to what she was asking of me. So I began to read more and I began to pray a *lot* more!

Don and Dotti

Over New Year's weekend, 2000, Bob and I hosted both Don and Dotti as our guests for the holiday. That weekend, Don told us he had told God years ago, "if being gay means I'm going to hell, then I guess I'm going to hell." At one time, our prayers for him were that he would leave the "gay lifestyle." Our prayers had changed over the last two or three years. We simply wanted him to reestablish his relationship with God.

I hoped and prayed that Don and Dotti would hit it off, and that maybe, just maybe, Dotti would be able to help Don reconnect with God.

Well, God was clearly at work that weekend. Don and Dotti were almost instantly friends. Five minutes after Dotti arrived, they discovered they were the same age, and their birthdays were just six weeks apart.

During that weekend, I entered into some of their conversations together, but also withdrew when I sensed the need for the two of them to be alone.

We also had some great fun with these two precious gifts from God that New Year's weekend. At that time, Dotti's family did not accept her sexual orientation. So we took some pictures of the two of them together, and Dotti exclaimed in here wonderful Atlanta/Lexington southern drawl: "Ah know what wee'll do, you take owa pictuah an' Ah'll send it to ma momma an' daddy an' tell'em this is mah new boyfriend!! That'll make 'em happy." The pictures turned out great!

Just hours after our holiday weekend with Don and Dotti ended, we received a phone call from Don who had arrived at his home in Chicago. I answered the phone and Don asked that Bob get on the line as well. And while trying to talk through his tears, he told us that he had just gone to his favorite spot along Lake Michigan, kneeled down and had asked God to take him back, and to use him as He saw fit. Life doesn't get any better than this—seeing God work before our very eyes, and having a long-term prayer answered. Our friend is continuing on with the Lord and has started going to church again.

Marsha

Through Dotti we came to know Marsha Stevens, a gay Christian singer, songwriter and performer. Marsha had written the song *"For Those Tears I Died,"* that had played at Anna's funeral. Anna had given me an autographed tape of Marsha's music titled *"Free to Be."* I was incensed when I received it; not believing Marsha could be both gay and Christian!

Mark Allen Powell writes about Marsha Stevens in an article from *Christian Century*, March 17, 1999: "Stevens is a nightmare for conservative Christians: she is a Jesus-loving, Bible-believing, God-fearing, lesbian Christian... Like many children of the Jesus Movement, Stevens had a troubled youth... she married young, thinking she had found a musical and spiritual soul mate. Seven years and two children later, the marriage ended. When her husband told her, 'You need to find someone else,' Stevens replied, 'You know, I think it might be a woman.' She was totally unprepared for what happened next. Christian singers had gotten divorced and had had babies out of wedlock, but the scandal that accompanied Steven's revelation of her sexual orientation was like no other: 'The Christian community excised me from its life,' she says. Some people from Stevens' church came over to insist she take the 'Jesus

Is Lord' sign off her door. People started ripping her songs out of their songbooks. The record company tried to deny her royalties, appealing to a 'backslider clause' in her contract that allowed such exclusion if she renounced the Christian faith. Fourteen months later, when her lover's daughter died of a congenital heart disease, Stevens was told it was divine vengeance and that her own children would be next. She wandered for awhile, trying to find a Christian home. 'The church didn't want me, but I just missed Jesus too much to stay away.' She'd sit in the back pews of a church until someone recognized her. Then she'd never return. To put bread on the table, she worked as a registered nurse."

Powell caught up with Marsha at the First Baptist Church in Granville, Ohio. He writes, "The concert in Granville was more a worship service than a gay pride rally. Her focus is on Jesus, to whom she sings hymns of praise. Still, she's open about who she is: a lesbian who loves the Lord. 'Don't let any church rob you of this treasure,' she tells the mostly gay audience. 'The gospel is for you. Jesus Christ is for you. Don't miss Christ because of Christians.'" Ouch!! Did Anna, who had known Marsha, miss Christ's unconditional love for her because of me?

Powell's article ends with: "...she repeatedly encounters what she calls 'identity theft.' So many gays have only negative associations with the word 'Christian.' Stevens assumes the burden of proof this brings. Gays and lesbians need to see Christians acting with love. 'Jesus did not say we'd be known by our righteous standards or low divorce rate or obedient children,' Stevens claims. 'He said we'd be known by our love.' On the other hand, the only way for gay and lesbian Christians to win the respect of the evangelical community is 'to let Jesus' love shine through us in ways that put our opponents to silence,' she says."

Dotti gave us a video of a Marsh Stevens's concert. We watched and listened to this beautiful, humorous, musically talented, openly gay Christian for one hour and forty-five minutes. I cried through much of it. How had I missed the boat here? Why did I not know about stuff like this? Had I been hiding my head in the sand? Had the evangelical Christian church been aware of this kind of thing, and simply chosen to ignore it? I was more moved by this concert than anything I had seen in recent months. Marsha loved the Lord—knew Him as her Savior, and likely had a closer walk with Christ than I did. Every song, every word of her video was like an arrow piercing my already fragmented heart once again.

There have been so many "arrows" in the past eight years. Jesus uses that concept in Hebrews 4:12: "For the Word of God is quick and powerful, and sharper than any two-edged sword, piercing even to the dividing asunder of soul and spirit, and of the joints and marrow, and is a discerner of the thoughts and intents of the heart." Even though the context of this verse is different than my experience during and after watching Marsha's video, the concept is true for me. Marsha's words pierced not only my heart, but also my soul and spirit.

Slowly, and carefully, God was removing the blinders from my eyes, readying me for the truths I had not yet been able to absorb.

Peggy and Tony

During the Lynchburg weekend, I had heard the name "Campolo" mentioned several times. I knew of Tony Campolo, but thought surely this must just be some coincidence. Someone with the same last name, but not related. It was beyond my imagination that the wife of an evangelistic speaker, writer and theologian, would be at that gathering, and a member of the Soulforce delegation, no less. But she was. My poor memory aided and abetted my confusion. I had forgotten about Tony's comments in Philip Yancey's book *What's So Amazing About Grace?*

And so, Bob and I had dinner with Peggy Campolo and a non-gay friend of hers from Pennsylvania, Kathy Stayton. I was puzzled. With seven of us in an Italian restaurant at 10:00 at night, it was impossible to figure out why she was there and where she stood.

It was only after I had returned home that I discovered why she was at the weekend in Virginia. A friend from church gave me a copy of the magazine, *The Other Side: Where Christians and Justice Embrace*. There was an article written by Peggy Campolo, called "The Holy Presence of Acceptance." Peggy and her husband Tony have different interpretations of Scripture. And, in fact, in this article, there is a sidebar that outlines their differences as follows:

Clarifying Our Differences

My husband, Tony Campolo, and I disagree at a crucial point on the subject of homosexual lifestyles. Because of his high profile in the Christian and evangelical world, it is only fair that I clarify these differences. I do not want him to be attacked for viewpoints that are mine.

We both believe that homosexual orientations are not chosen any more than heterosexual orientations are chosen. We agree that the term "homosexual lifestyle" is a misnomer—there are as many homosexual lifestyles, as there are heterosexual lifestyles. We oppose promiscuous lifestyles, which use and discard people.

Tony and I believe that homosexual people should not have to be "in the closet" to be part of the body of Christ and we are saddened that the church has done so little to include homosexual people.

We both are angered by the terrible lies about gays and lesbians propagated by some church leaders, lies that have led to cruel mistreatment and great injustice. We both pray for the church to repent.

We differ on the issue of monogamous, loving relationships between people of the same sex. While we both believe such relationships should be legally permissible in a pluralistic society, I enthusiastically affirm such relationships for Christians. Tony does not.

I support Tony's right to his beliefs, even as I am very grateful that he has, at considerable personal cost, supported my right to mine. I have been with him in places where his views on homosexuality put him so far to the left that he is viewed as an enemy by many in the church. He has received letters of condemnation and phone calls from evangelical leaders pressuring him to change his stance. I am proud that he has stood up for his convictions on the subject of homosexuality in places where it is far more difficult for him than it is for me to share my words here in The Other Side.

Well now. What was I to do with this information? Tony Campolo had spoken at our church that summer. We all loved and respected him. I decided to write the following letter to Peggy:

Dear Peggy,

The Lynchburg weekend was life changing for both my husband and me. We were honored to have met you and enjoyed dinner with you.

I'll get right to the point: I'm being challenged, gently, by Dotti and Mel, to "do my homework" and figure out what the Bible really says about homosexuality, and what I really believe.

Peggy, I am not a theologian. Are you willing to share with me your perspective on the passages in Scripture, particularly I Corinthians 6:9, and Romans 1? Right now, I'm pretty confused about what I believe, except for the fact that I know I personally have only two responsibilities toward all people, including gays and lesbians. I am to love them and pray for them. It is only God who changes lives as He sees fit and they are willing, and that includes everyone, not just GLBTs.

Maybe because of my story, I hurt desperately for these people, and have come to love them dearly. But, I grew up in a very legalistic environment—Plymouth Brethren (exclusive, not open) and have some difficulty re-recording some of those old tapes that often play in my head.

I'd be most grateful for whatever help you could give me. Bob and I have such high regard for both you and Tony. We value your opinion greatly.

Thanks in advance,
Mary Lou Wallner

Well, imagine my surprise when I received a *very* long letter from Peggy in return. She also sent me a couple of tapes. One of which I've listened to four times. It is from a chapel service discussion at North Park University in Chicago on February 29, 1996. Tony and Peggy are discussing their views, and their hearts on this issue. I *listened* when Tony said, "We sing 'Just As I Am' and mean it for everybody but gay people." I *listened* when Tony said, "I am *not* approving of homosexual activity. I am *disapproving* of a Church that does not love people who Jesus will NEVER STOP LOVING!!" If you have ever heard Tony Campolo speak, you know that the capital letters in that sentence match the unmistakable timbre of his voice. It was downright *loud*!

During that chapel service discussion, Peggy makes one statement that stands out in my mind. I've repeated her comment to many others, as I hand them a copy of the cassette tape. Peggy says that the term "homosexual lifestyle" is a misnomer. She quips that she and Madonna are both heterosexuals, but their lifestyles are vastly different. And then she smiles and says, "I can't sing."

I then remembered that Jesus said, "Love your enemies." The gay Christian is not my enemy. That person simply needs my love and my prayers, just like I need theirs.

In Peggy's letter, she recommended that I read several books. (I'm still working on that.) Then she went on to write a paragraph that affected me profoundly. She writes:

Mary Lou, I cannot fathom the pain and sadness you know because you must wait until the life after this one to talk to your own daughter. But I see in the searching you are doing, the most wonderful memorial you could build for her. She is fine—a child of God who is finally Home; it is you who hurt and feel loss. She has perfect understanding now, even of things that those who loved her did that hurt her because they didn't understand who she was.

By coming to places like Lynchburg, and being willing to tell your story, you make things clear to a lot of people who wouldn't listen to Mel or me, but who have to listen to you. Thank you, my friend, and know that I am honored to be your friend, and eager to be of any help I can be.

There was another paragraph in Peggy's letter that simply delighted me, and believe me, I still look for anything that will do that, in the midst of my sorrow over losing Anna. She writes:

Incidentally, Mary Lou, I know a family down south who are Plymouth Brethren, and very strict. A "biggie" with them is not to wear earrings! Their son felt led to become a Baptist minister, and they act as though he is a card dealer in Las Vegas, finding it impossible to celebrate his ministry. I always wonder if people like that ever feel or are guided by the Holy Spirit when they act that way. I really don't think God stopped interacting with people when the Bible was given to us. I believe the light is still unfolding, and that God is guiding our hearts today. And Mary Lou, even given the chance that I could be wrong about some things, I would rather err on the side of love.

And then I began to ponder this delightful and articulate lady named Peggy. I read her story in a booklet we received that weekend in Lynchburg. This is what it said:

For as long as I can remember, I have believed that homosexual people are entitled to all the rights and privileges enjoyed by those of us who are heterosexual, including the right to have their committed partnerships recognized both by the church and the state. I have always considered sexual orientation in the same way that I consider the fact that while most people are right-handed people, some people are left-handed. I know that left-handed people used to be persecuted in this country, and I longed for the day when we would be as enlightened about sexual orientation as we are now about handedness.

There were many times in my life when I wanted to take a stand on the issue of homosexuality, but it was not until I had a personal encounter with Jesus Christ fifteen years ago, that I found the courage to speak out for my gay brothers and lesbian sisters. Standing with them is the place where I know God wants me to be.

The Bible tells us that Jesus was always willing to stand with those who were rejected and treated as outcasts. I would like to see more church leaders do that for homosexual people. Dr. Falwell is a very influential man, and I pray that one day soon he will truly come to know who God's gay and lesbian children are, and speak out for them. There is no text about homosexual orientation in the Bible, but the Bible has plenty to say about God's grace to all people and God's call to justice and mercy.

In this same booklet, Peggy's biography reads as follows:

Peggy Campolo is a writer and editor. She is a graduate of Eastern College, and taught first grade prior to spending a number of years as a full-time wife and mother. Mrs. Campolo has worked in real estate and public relations. She belongs to PFLAG (Parents, Families and Friends of Lesbians and Gays), is a working member of Evangelicals Concerned, and serves on the Council of the Association of Welcoming and Affirming Baptists. She has spoken at churches, colleges and conferences throughout the United States. Mrs. Campolo and her husband live in St. David's, Pennsylvania. They are the parents of two grown children and have four grandchildren.

Whew! I began to wonder. The Campolo's chapel message was in my own city, and took place almost exactly one year before Anna's death. *Why* had I not heard any of this before? The information was *out there*!! *Why* did I not know about it in time to save Anna's life? What if just one year earlier, I had heard the tape by Tony and Peggy? Maybe, just maybe, Anna would still be alive. Was the reason I did not hear about this, or know about it, my own fault? Probably. Does the church bear any responsibility? Most likely. All the churches I have attended over the years, usually stayed away from the topic of homosexuality. It was too volatile an issue—and still is. I am learning that this issue seems to define whether a person is "evangelical" or not. I have not heard the subject tackled very often from the pulpit, but when it is, it could always be summed up in one-sentence: Homosexuality is a sin. There was never any information surrounding the topic, nor was there any talk about "homosexuality" as opposed to the term "homosexual activity."

Once again, slowly, ever so slowly, and carefully, God was lifting the veil from my tear-filled eyes.

Julio

In my work as an HIV nurse, I met many wonderful people. One of them was Bruce. He loved the Lord and knew Him as Savior. Bruce frequently attended a Love In Action Bible Study, which is a Christian support group for people with HIV and AIDS. Bruce also took charge of his care, and disease process. He refused traditional medicines and chose instead to use herbal remedies and alternative therapies.

On February 5, 1998, Bruce was hospitalized with PCP—Pneumocystis Carinii Pneumonia, an opportunistic infection peculiar to people with HIV. He was in intensive care for 4 days. He was released from the hospital on antibiotics, and outwardly, was doing better. The date? February 10, 1998.

But something was not right. Bruce came to our clinic to see the physician on Tuesday, February 25. His gait was funny, almost like he was drunk, only he did not drink. The physician, Dr. Judith Nerad, an Infectious Disease Specialist, is a very lovely, compassionate, intelligent lady. She ordered an MRI of the brain for Bruce—to be done immediately. The results came back as "unidentified lesions in the white matter."

I will never forget what happened the next day. Bruce's case manager and I went to see him and fill his medicine boxes for him (with the HIV regimen prescribed by Dr. Nerad). After the bout with PCP, Bruce had agreed to try some HIV medicines. When we got to his and Julio's apartment, actually the second story of a big old house, we noted that Bruce had further declined, was having trouble speaking clearly, and his gait was even more wobbly. I paged Dr. Nerad and she said to take him right to the emergency room. And so, Bruce was readmitted to the hospital on February 26, 1998.

Bruce was released on March 6, 1998. The conclusion the physicians had reached was that Bruce had the JC Virus. This virus is rare, but often associated with a depressed immune system, and causes a serious brain disorder called PML (for those of you who are medically inclined, PML stand for Progressive Multifocal Leukoencephalopathy.) *That's* a mouthful!! My Merck Manual says, "No treatment has proved effective."

One physician said he might live 6-12 months. Another said he might only last a few weeks. But what actually came to pass were 25 days of sheer terror for Bruce and Julio, and great sadness for all of us at the clinic.

We all watched Bruce decline very rapidly. I remember going to see Bruce and Julio one Saturday afternoon, and Bruce was bed-ridden and could barely be understood. He had already been signed up with Hospice, but I knew of an in-patient hospice 12-bed unit in a hospital about 17 miles away. I phoned Bruce's physician, and he gave the order to have Bruce transferred there. I had been a hospice nurse for the same organization that ran this particular unit. I phoned them, and arranged for an ambulance to transfer Bruce that day, March 25, 1998.

Julio was at his side almost constantly. The nurses in the Hospice Unit at Alexian Brothers Medical Center were wonderful. They allowed Julio to move the two single beds in the room together and further told Julio that he could sleep in the bed next to Bruce.

On March 31, 1998, Bruce slipped into a coma, and at 9:55 a.m., he went to be with his Lord. I will never forget asking Bruce, while he was still at home, "Bruce, when you die, do you know where you're going?" He said, "Yes, I do! I'm going to heaven." I showed him a picture of Anna and asked him to look her up and give her a hug and kiss for me. He said he would do just that.

But, then there were pieces to be picked up—namely Julio. We knew that Bruce (or Brucie as Julio called him) had been the love of his life. How was I to minister to this dear Cuban-born gay man? I didn't really have a clue, but God did. Julio knew about Anna, and therefore, he knew that I knew what grief was all about. Julio and I talked almost daily for about two months.

Shortly after Bruce's death, we invited Julio to go to our church, Willow Creek, with us for a weekend service and then later, to the mid-week service. We knew that our large church (with many small groups) could provide comfort and healing to those who are grieving. We also prayed that Julio would be able to receive that special compassion that only God can give. Julio accepted our invitation. We were later to find out that he really wanted nothing to do with what he termed "right wing evangelical Christian fundamentalists." When Bruce was going to the Love In Action Bible Study, the leader once came to Bruce and Julio's home, and in no uncertain terms, told Julio that he was a sinner and condemned to hell because he was a homosexual. So Julio's hesitancy was understandable. Plus the fact, that Julio, when he was 17, wanted to be a Catholic priest, and entered the seminary to do just that. Someone *told* on him—someone who was also gay. But Julio was the one asked to leave the seminary, and his chosen vocation. Julio had very little use for organized religion but he continued to join us each week at Willow Creek Community Church. And, he came to love our church as we did.

And then, one Tuesday in December of 1999, Julio called me at work "just to make sure" we were all planning to go to New Community (the mid-week service) the next night. This was and odd call, because even though we touch base every week before Wednesday night, his call made me think he had something special in mind. And he did.

Julio decided (finally—the day before) to tell us that he was going to be baptized at Willow Creek the next evening. I think people at the other end of my office probably heard my *shout* of sheer joy that arose from my lips and my heart, as I took this in. Okay, now. Here we have a gay Christian, who is going to be baptized in our church. What did all this mean? What did the future hold, for Julio, for us, and for Willow Creek? But before I even attempt to answer those questions, please enjoy the testimony that Julio wrote:

If someone had told me two years ago that I would today have a personal relationship with Jesus and would be writing a testimony for a Baptism, I'd have told them that they were greatly mistaken.

Though I was raised in a Catholic home, my parents read the Bible, and I even attended the seminary for two years of high school and two years of college. I felt God was distant to me and continued searching. I went to a variety of churches over the years including Lutheran, Episcopal, and even became a Buddhist for several years. I became more and more disillusioned with every church I attended, and eventually became so cynical that if I met someone and they said anything about "being reborn" or "family values," I wanted nothing to do with them. I continued to believe in God and in Jesus, but I did not go to church at all, and my religion became my own private thing.

My life was going well and I was happy, though I knew something was missing. Then in March 1998, my life became a drunken spiral into darkness. I was angry and resentful and felt completely alone. After almost five years of sobriety, I started drinking uncontrollably. I did not want to go on living. A nurse I met through my partner's illness invited me to the weekend service at Willow. I figured I had nothing to lose at this point.

I went and realized this was like no church I had ever attended. I soon began to go to Willow with my friend and her husband. I went every Wednesday, and the worship and message sustained me from week to week. I felt God was looking out for me and reaching out to me, so I responded. In May 1998, I made my commitment to Christ and accepted the gift of redemption and salvation. Since then, my life has improved on a daily basis. The darkness has given way to support, and God has seen to it that I have all I need to survive.

My life now is totally different than it was before I made the commitment to have Christ in my life. Though I still have problems and worries, I know I am not alone, and have a Savior and a friend in the Lord. I have made changes in my thinking and my behavior, and at 46, I have the relationship with God that I searched for my whole life. I am filled with gratitude to God for literally saving my life.

Julio struggled mightily about inviting his parents to his baptism. He was concerned that they would think that his infant baptism in the Catholic church did not "take." Julio is very close to his parents, especially his mom. They have been a part of his struggles with alcoholism for many years. We suggested that maybe they would like to be a part of a *good* thing that was happening in his life. So, Julio mustered his courage, called his folks and invited them to his baptism. They came, and had dinner with us and a group of our friends, at the church before the service.

Julio wanted us to go up on the platform with him, and he wanted our mid-week teaching pastor, John Ortberg, to baptize him. There are usually a very large number that are baptized in our church twice a year. In fact, in the summer of 1999, over 900 people were baptized. Sort of reminds me of Acts 2:41 which says, "Those who accepted [Peter's] message were baptized, and about three thousand were added to their number that day."

Early on in his attendance at Willow, Julio wrote John Ortberg a note of appreciation, and John wrote back, "Just keep coming."

To our thrill and amazement, it was Julio's testimony that was read over the loud speaker during the baptism ceremony. They did not leave out the word "partner." Could it be that Willow Creek was trying to do as Jesus did and love everyone, regardless?

We did go up on the platform with Julio, and waited in a long line of people who wanted John to baptize them. All those that were being baptized had name tags on, so when we arrived in front of John, he simply said *"Julio!"* John knew who this man was, asked who we were, and proceeded to ask Julio if he knew Jesus Christ to be the Savior and Lord of his life. Julio answered yes, and John baptized him. I don't know who was most thrilled at that moment: Julio, John or my husband and I!

After the evening was over, Julio's mother thanked us for all we had done for Julio, and I simply said to her, "You laid the groundwork—you get the credit."

David

The name, David, is in my family. I have a brother named David and also two brothers-in-law. After Anna's death, Bob and I went through a grief support workshop at our church. Several months later, we decided to volunteer in this ministry, as small group leaders. Naturally, we had been given a group of people, many of whom, had lost a loved one to suicide. In our first group, we had the mother of an 18-year old young man who fell from a 400 foot cable tower, and the cousin of a woman who (along with two of her children) was murdered. It was a difficult experience, being small group leaders to these dear survivors.

Another member of our team was a man named David. He was the leader of the small group leaders. The church has a rule: "Everyone is cared for and no one cares for more than ten." David's title was *Coach*.

Each week before the workshop session, David met with the small group leaders to see how things were going, give announcements, and ask for prayer requests. I was inexplicably drawn to David.

I have always loved the story of David in the Bible. He made lots of mistakes, like when he slept with Bathsheba, got her pregnant, and then had her husband, Uriah, killed in battle. And still, throughout Scripture, God's love for David is profoundly evident. Acts 13:22 says, "After removing Saul, He [God] made David their king. He testified concerning him: 'I have found David, son of Jesse, a man after my own heart; he will do everything I want him to do.'"

This particular David, from the church, came to be an incredibly kind, sensitive and wonderful friend.

After the first two workshop sessions, I decided to take a hiatus from leading a small group in Grief Support at the church. During the summer of 1999, I thought I was ready to return, and I spent about an hour talking with David about doing so. And then, something else happened. I was informed of a new ministry starting at the church. It was to be geared to those who are "struggling" with homosexuality. I expressed an interest in this, and finally decided to be part of the start-up team. I then had the unpleasant task of informing David that I would not be coming back to Grief Support after all. I explained the reason to him.

There was a very long silence at the other end of the phone. Finally David spoke: "I have struggled with homosexuality for 36 years." I was stunned…and yet not so stunned. I then clearly understood why I was so drawn to him nearly a year earlier. I also knew that David had been diagnosed with obsessive-compulsive disorder, and manic-depression. At the time, David had been married for 22 years, and had only come out to his wife about 6 years earlier.

We invited David and his wife to come to our home for dinner. David came alone—feeling that this first meeting with our new knowledge of him might be better off done with just him present and not his wife.

And what a story he had to tell! He had grown up in a rather dysfunctional family, and his parents were both deceased. He had not had a good relationship with them when they were alive. He went on to tell us about his orientation (developmental, he believes). He had had a difficult relationship with a boss; difficult, because David fell in love with him. But David was also married, and so was this man. Both men were part of our church at the time.

David had decided to live a life of homosexual celibacy. Whether or not he is gifted with celibacy is unimportant. This is the choice he has made—to honor his vows to his wife.

David also became part of the start-up team for the new ministry. He reads me like a book! When we were in meetings together, it was almost eerie. I could be sitting in a chair, saying nothing, but with my emotions teeming, and thinking I am not exhibiting any body language at all, and David would call on me and say, "Okay, what's up, Mary Lou? Your body language is screaming."

I love him dearly, and count him one of my most valuable friends. He once told me that what keeps him alive, is looking into the eyes of people attending the Grief Support workshops, especially those who have lost a loved one to suicide. He states that visualizing the pain and misery in the faces of these dear people is something he does not want to put anyone through. He is alive, and I thank God for that!

Lewis

And then there was Lewis Smedes. I mentioned him earlier in a quote that he wrote about Mel White's book, *Stranger at the Gate*. I had heard him speak twice to the New Community service at Willow Creek Community Church. John Ortberg, the teaching pastor who baptized Julio, referred to Dr. Smedes as his "mentor."

A friend from church told me Dr. Smedes had an article on the Soulforce website (www.soulforce.org). I thought this gal was kidding me. Surely a theologian of his experience and reputation could not be promoting an organization like Soulforce, or allow any of his writings to be part of that website. But, once again, I was wrong. I checked it out. It was true. Lew Smedes had an article on the Soulforce website entitled, "Like the Wideness of the Sea." In this article, he likens the attitude of the church towards homosexuals to the attitude of the church towards divorced and remarried people some years ago. Read on, and really *hear* what Dr. Smedes is saying. He writes:

> ...*Which brings me to the question that I wish to raise: Was the church's embrace of people who were once divorced and are now living faithfully in second marriages a precedent for embracing homosexual people who live faithfully in covenanted*

partnerships?

To answer this question, we must answer two others first. The first question is this: Is a partnership of two homosexual persons morally similar—in relevant ways—to the marriage of divorced and remarried heterosexual people? The second question we must answer is this: Does the Bible's word about homosexuals lay down a rule for excluding partnered Christian homosexuals from the church's fellowship? Or does it witness to God's original intention for sexual orientation without laying down abiding rules for the church? How can we find the answers to these two questions?

It seems to me that the only way to answer the first question is to take a good look at what is really going on with partnered Christian homosexuals and then compare what we see in them to what we have seen in remarried heterosexuals. And the only way to answer the second question is to go back and study the Bible's teaching on homosexual behavior in the light of what we have discerned about what was really going on when homosexual people committed themselves to a monogamous partnership. In short, we have to do the same thing the church did when it decided to embrace remarried people.

Are the two situations significantly and relevantly like each other? Let me share ways in which I think they are.

Both divorced and remarried partners and homosexual partners are seeking to fulfill a fundamental, God-implanted human need for a shared life of intimate, committed and exclusive love with one other human being.

Both are fulfilling their God-given human need in the only way available to them, not what the Creator originally intended for his children, but the only way they have.

Both are striving to do the one thing the Lord considered supremely important about all sexual relationships: they are living their sexual lives within their covenants with each other. Both are trying to create the best lives they can within the limits of personal conditions they cannot change. Both want to live as followers of Christ within the supportive embrace of the Church.

It seems to me, therefore, that the moral and spiritual situations of divorced and remarried heterosexuals and the situation of homosexuals in a covenanted partnership are significantly similar. Enough alike, at any rate, to lead us into the second question: Is the biblical basis for excluding partnered Christian homosexuals any stronger or clearer than it was for excluding divorced and remarried heterosexuals? I suggest that we examine just one passage, Romans 1:18-27, the text most scholars agree is the New Testament's most definitive judgment on homosexual behavior.

In this passage, Paul tells us that God had abandoned people who refused to worship and give him thanks for his gifts. These God-forsaken people—bereft of the restraining presence of God—lapsed into a swarm of deplorable behaviors with which most of us are experientially familiar. Some of them fell into unnatural homosexual lusts with which most of us have had no personal experience. (Mind now, God did not abandon them because they had done such things. They did them because God had abandoned them.)

Who were these people, the ones who were having sex with partners of their own gender? Temple prostitutes? Pederasts? People engaged in wild orgies? Nobody knows for sure. But it seems to me that we can be certain of who they were not: they were not the sorts of people that I am talking about in this essay—Christian homosexual persons who are living out their need for abiding love in monogamous and covenanted partnerships of love. Three things about these people tell me that the apostle could not have been talking about them.

The people Paul has in mind had refused to acknowledge and worship God and for this reason were abandoned by God to their lustful depravity.

The people I am talking about have not rejected God at all; they love God and they thank God for his grace and his gifts. How, then, could they have been abandoned to homosexuality as a punishment for refusing to acknowledge God?

The people Paul speaks of had turned form "natural" heterosexual practices to homosexual practices. The Christian homosexuals that I am talking about have not given up heterosexual passions for homosexual lusts. They have never been heterosexual. They have been homosexual from the moment of their earliest sexual stirrings.

The people Paul had in mind were constantly lusting after each other and in their actions were only following their lusts. The homosexual people I am talking about do not lust after each other any more than heterosexual people lust after each other. They seek abiding personal companionship, enduring love, shared intimacy and complete trust from each other just as heterosexual people, at their best, do. Their love for one another is likely to be just as spiritual and personal as any heterosexual love can be.

Hold on, wait just a minute, a sharp reader may say: "You ignore the fact that Paul said that these people were doing something contrary to nature. If what they did was contrary to nature in Paul's day, it must still be contrary to nature today. And their sexual practice does not become more natural by doing it in monogamous partnerships. Remarried heterosexual people's second marriage sex is natural. So what makes the cases essentially different from each other is that one is natural and the other is unnatural."

Well, Paul certainly did consider the sorts of homosexual behavior that he had observed (or heard about) to be "contrary to nature." But what he meant by "contrary to nature," none of us knows for sure. The traditional Catholic and Reformed view has been that it was contrary to nature because, to be natural, sex had to be capable of conceiving children—a view derived reasonably enough from the simple biblical story of how God created his children. Therefore, homosexual relations are not natural and, being unnatural, they are essentially different from and much worse than the sexual relationships of remarried heterosexuals.

But not many modern Evangelical Protestants believe that only baby-making sex is natural. Most believe that God meant sex to be the most intimate way to express love within a committed partnership. To be consistent, then, modern evangelicals would have to agree that, at least on this score, homosexual relations within committed love can be as true to nature as are heterosexual relations within committed love.

The whole argument would be avoided, some say, if homosexuals were willing to be celibate. When the church asks homosexual Christians to be celibate, they say, it asks no more of them than it asks of any single heterosexual person. But in fact it does ask more, much more of homosexual people. To single people in general it says: you must choose between celibacy and marriage. But to all homosexuals it says: you have no choice; you may not marry and you must be celibate.

The apostle conceded that most heterosexual people did not have the gift to be celibate. Such people, he said, were free to get married even though celibacy might have been more ideal for them (1 Corinthians 7: 8,9). If Paul thought that most heterosexual people lacked the gift of celibacy would he not have thought that at least some homosexuals lack it?

In sum, then, the promiscuous and lust-driven people Paul was talking about in his letter to the Romans could not have been, it seems to me, Christian homosexual people who—being left with no better option—choose to live together in covenanted partnerships. And the biblical ground for excluding them from embrace within the church is actually weaker than was its ground for excluding divorced and remarried heterosexuals.

Early on, back when I was talking about divorced and remarried people, I mentioned three shifts in the church's consciousness that were going on behind the scenes and preparing the way for their embrace by the church. Let me recall them. For one thing, the church became sensitive to the growing number of divorces and remarriages among their own sons and daughters. For another, the church began to see and feel the sacrament more as medicine for our spiritual illness than as a symptom of our spiritual health. And thirdly, the church became more aware that it could not tell how the Lord's Word about marriage should be applied to real people unless the church also had eyes for the real people it affected.

It seems to me that our attitudes toward Christian homosexual partners are being modulated these days in exactly the same way. And I wonder whether the changes might be preparing us for the consideration of a new policy of embrace just as they did half a century ago.

We have, in the first place, begun to see the "homosexual problem" in the faces of beloved homosexual persons who are our own or our friends; sons and daughters. We have, in the second place, become more sensitive to the sacrament as a support for Christians who are trying to do the Lord's will for them even though the Lord's ideal is out of their reach. And, thirdly, we have begun to see that we need to factor our discernment of what is really going on with partnered Christian homosexual people into our understanding of the Lord's will for the church's policy toward them.

Recall that I began this long discussion by asking this question: Does the church's dramatic move from the exclusion to the embrace of divorced and remarried Christians provide a precedent for an embrace of homosexual Christians who live together in a committed partnership?

My own answer to my own questions is, yes, it does seem to me that our embrace of divorced and remarried Christian people did indeed set a precedent for embracing Christian homosexuals who live together. And I am here and there, as mothers and fathers of homosexual people tell me their stories, picking up signs of hope that eventually the church will see it as I—and they—do.

This is the end of my argument. Before I quit, however, I need to make a couple of personal remarks.

Some homosexuals feel devalued when people like me say that their orientation and their way of life in not how the Creator originally intended his sexual children to live out their sexuality. They say that their homosexuality is as at home in and native to God's creation as heterosexuality is. Some say that it is God's special gift for them to celebrate and thank him for, just as their sexuality is a gift for heterosexuals to celebrate. I cannot believe it is. I have not found quite the right word for it, but it seems to me that homosexuality is a burden that some of God's children are called on to bear, an anomaly; nature gone awry. But I do believe that homosexuality is the only raw material they have for living as good a life of sexual love as they can within our broken world where so much of life is bent out of shape.

I believe that God blesses us when we improvise on nature's lapses. To create my own family, for instance, three mothers had to have given away their own children. And my children had to suffer the deep trauma of being torn away, long before their time, from their mothers. Surely Doris' and my way of family making was not part of God's design for the family. But I know that he gives his supportive grace to such improvised families as mine. And, in the same way, I believe, he gives his supportive grace to the way homosexuals improvise marriage-like covenants for themselves even though they cannot by sexual means create families.

Some time ago, an elderly couple of a fundamentalist persuasion told me about their fear for their daughter's soul. She had left their church because she could no longer accept some of its fundamentalist demands on her life. The daughter still confesses Christ as her Savior, but her parents consider her denial of some fundamentalist standards an equivalent to a denial of the Lord. Their sorrow and fear for their daughter made me very sad. And, as happens to me often these days when I feel sad, a hymn popped into my head as a kind of antidepressant: "There's a wideness in God's mercy like the wideness of the sea."

My church's exclusion of homosexuals who confess Christ and live together in committed love makes me very sad in the same way. And when I think about it, I am haunted by the same hymn. Is there really a wideness in God's mercy like the wideness of the sea? Is his mercy wide enough for people who, through no choice of their own, have no other way to fulfill one of the deepest of all human needs but the way that my wife and I have fulfilled them for fifty years—in an abiding partnership of lasting love? I think I know my own heart well enough to believe that if his mercy is wide enough for me, it must be wide enough for them. (Lewis Smedes as printed in the www.soulforce.org website)

I was so *struck* by Dr. Smedes' article that I had to look up the hymn. It goes like this:

There's Wideness in God's Mercy
Wellesley
Frederick W. Faber/Lizzie S. Tourjee

There's a wideness in God's mercy, like the
wideness of the sea;
There's a kindness in His justice, which is
more than liberty
There's a welcome for the sinner, and more
Graces for the good;
There is mercy with the Savior;
There is healing in His blood.
For the love of God is broader than the
Measure of man's mind;
And the heart of the Eternal is most
Wonderfully kind.
If our love were but more simple, we
Should take Him at His Word.
And our lives would be all sunshine in
the sweetness of our Lord.

(Quoted from *The New Church Hymnal,* © 1976 by Lexicon Music, Inc.)

And yes, you guessed it. I had to write Lew Smedes a letter, too:

November 14, 1999

Dear Dr. Smedes,

My husband and I are participating members of Willow Creek Community Church and have heard you speak the past two summers at New Community. We have SO appreciated your words to us.

*Through an amazing set of circumstances, we found ourselves in Lynchburg, Virginia the weekend of October 22-24, 1999—at Mel White's invitation and expense. We had read his book **Stranger At The Gate** and emailed him with our story, thanking him for helping us understand the struggle. He asked us to come and tell our story that weekend. We received counsel from four godly people whom we trusted. Two of these people were John Ortberg and Philip Yancey. John was a teaching pastor of Willow Creek Community Church, and Philip Yancey is editor-at-large for Christianity Today magazine. We agreed to go.*

*Just today, we went into the Soulforce website and discovered your article **Like The Wideness of the Sea**. Dr. Smedes, you can't possibly know how much that article has helped clarify our thinking. Thank you so much. I grew up in a very rigid, legalistic environment (exclusive Plymouth Brethren) and continue to struggle to rid myself of those old "tapes." Your article helped so much.*

And so, I thought you might like to read my story. It's very sad. I wish I could go back and change it all, but I cannot. But maybe, because of my story, some lives will be saved. I've started to write a book about all of this but don't know if there will be a market for it anywhere. Anyway, here's the talk I gave three times in Lynchburg.

[…]

Dr. Smedes, thank you for reading this. I would welcome any response you might have.

Lewis Smedes emailed me with the following response:

Dear Mary Lou,

Your letter has filled my spirit with pain for you and outrage at the church's cruel mistreatment of its gay children. What a horror in your life!! What desperate and abysmal pain your daughter had to live with! It just twists my soul into a tight knot. You know that your main healing comes from the grace of God; I hope that it has gradually brought you back to a bit of joy.

*I have just returned from a five-week absence and have a mountain of correspondence to care for and a trip to Jordan and Palestine next week where I must talk about reconciliation. So you will have to bear with a certain brevity. I do not usually recommend my own books to people, but if you have not read my **Forgive And Forget** or **The Art of Forgiving**, I urge you to get one or both of them and read at least the chapters on forgiving ourselves.*

Bless you.
Lewis Smedes

Henri Nouwen

According to Balswick and Balswick in the book *Authentic Human Sexuality: An Integrated Christian Approach* (InterVarsity Press, Downers Grove, IL), "Erotic sexual activity between same-sex persons has occurred throughout recorded history. According to Scanzoni and Mollenkott (1978) the following well-known people may have had a lifelong homosexual orientation: Erasmus (1466-1536), a scholar and editor of the Greek New Testament; Leonardo de Vinci (1452-1519), the artist who gifted the world with the moving portrait of Christ in *The Last Supper*; James I of England (1566-1625) who commissioned the translation of the bible that bears his name *The Kind James Version (KJV)*; Michelangelo (1475-1564) who created the beautiful sculpture *The Pieta* as well as the magnificent frescoes on the ceilings of the Sistine Chapel; Sir Frances Bacon (1521-1626), an outstanding essayist and scientific theorist; Mary II (1662-1694), Queen of England, Scotland and Ireland; Walt Whitman (1819-1892), the famous American poet; Peter Ilyich Tchaikovsky (1840-1916), the great composer; and Henry James (1843-1916), an American novelist." (pp. 32-37)

And then there is Henri Nouwen (1932-1996) who was often quoted in sermons by the pastors at Willow Creek.

My dear friend, Linda—the one who loaned me *Stranger at the Gate*, and whose twin died of AIDS—gave me Henri Nouwen's book *The Inner Voice of Love: A Journey Through Anguish to Freedom*. In the flyleaf, my friend wrote:

> Mary Lou—The path of spiritual growth may lead one through "the dark night of the soul." This is not punishment, rejection or abandonment...though it may appear to be. It is a divine appointment with the grace of God. It is a time when one must wait on God. Depression, dryness, lostness, despair are all part of the path. If we hang on even by our fingertips, we will come to see that God has lovingly taken us to a higher place so we can see Him more clearly—a place we could never reach on our own. At long last we are amazed by His grace—bringing good out of what was intended for evil. Not every wounded one chooses this path to freedom. Many fear it greatly—and with reason. That they run away is not surprising. You and I have chosen (were chosen?) to walk this path and we will never be the same.
> Thank you, Father.

Nouwen was a Catholic priest and taught in several theological institutes and universities in his home country (The Netherlands) and in the United States. A man by the name of Michael Ford has written a book about Nouwen's life, called *Wounded Prophet*. In an article about his book in the magazine *Open Hands*, Ford states: "Nouwen, who was gay himself, first recognized his sexual orientation at the same time as he started responding to his call to the priesthood—at the age of six. For much of his life he agonized over what for him was clearly a conflict: he was passionate about people and even suffered a complete emotional breakdown after one platonic friendship collapsed because of the expectations he had of it. During the last decade of his life at L'Arche (a community of people living with disabilities and abilities), he slowly came to accept his sexual identity and showed particular kindness to fellow homosexual Christians, especially those in relationships he described as 'holy.' (Vol. 15, No.2, Fall 1999, page 25).

I was deeply moved by Nouwen's book *The Inner Voice of Love*… It spoke volumes to my heart and my inner spirit. Allow me to quote a few parts from his book. Nouwen writes, "To my surprise, I never lost the ability to write. In fact, writing became part of my struggle for survival. It gave me the little distance from myself that I needed to keep from drowning in my despair" (P. xvi).

I, too, have journaled since June of 1997—four months after Anna died. Nouwen described my pain to a "T" when he stated, "There is a deep hole in your being, like an abyss. You will never succeed in filling that hole, because your needs are inexhaustible. You have to work around it so that gradually the abyss closes…There are two extremes to avoid: being completely absorbed in your pain and being distracted by so many things that you stay far away from the wound you want to heal." (P. 31)

I have many times described my anguish as a deep hole in the center of my being that just cannot seem to get closed up.

One emotion that often brings great pain to my soul is emptiness. Nouwen says, "You have to begin to trust that your experience of emptiness is not the final experience, that beyond it is a place where you are being held in love. As long as you do not trust that place beyond your emptiness, you cannot safely reenter the place of pain." (p.26) I made a note in the book at this point, dated December 29, 1997. I wrote, "If the new place beyond my emptiness is 'being held in love,' I'm not there yet. I *still* don't *feel* loved, or in any way worthy of *being* loved." Self-esteem, or lack thereof, remains an issue for me. I wonder if it will ever be healthy again, this side of heaven, or even if it ever was healthy!

Friendships have been especially difficult for me since Anna's death. I have had a distinct personality change since her death and am more melancholy than ever before. Most people I know do not want to be around someone who is grieving. At times, I laugh and have fun, but my needs are for deeper and more meaningful relationships, not those that are superficial. Nouwen speaks to this when he says, "The love that came to you in particular, concrete human friendships and that awakened your dormant desire to be completely and unconditionally loved was real and authentic. It does not have to be denied as dangerous and idolatrous. A love that comes to you through human beings is true, God-given love and needs to be celebrated as such. When human friendships prove to be unlivable because you demand that your friends love you in ways that are beyond human capacity, you do not have to deny the reality of the love you received. When you try to die to that love in order to find God's love, you are doing something God does not want. The task is not to die to life-giving relationships but to realize that the love you received in them is part of a greater love…So stop trying to die to the particular real love you have received. Be grateful for it and see it as what enabled you to open yourself to God's first love." (p.28-29)

I need to hear these words well, and heed them. Often, my expectations of how others should befriend me is simply not realistic. It does not help that a year after Anna died, two friends expressed surprise that I was not "over it" yet. Another new friend wrote me saying she did not think our new friendship was "working." Maybe my expectations of her were too great and drove her away. I felt sad about it. Nouwen says it better than I: "Be sure that God will truly fulfill all your needs. Keep remembering that. It will help you not to expect that fulfillment from people who you already know are incapable of giving it." (P. 43)

Another emotion I struggle with is loneliness. Nouwen writes: "It is not easy to stay with your loneliness. The temptation is to nurse your pain or to escape into fantasies about people who will take it away. But when you can acknowledge your loneliness in a safe contained place, you make your pain available for God's healing…It is important that you dare to stay with your pain and allow it to be there. You have to own your loneliness and trust that it will not always be there. The pain you suffer now is meant to put you in touch with the place where you most need healing, your very heart…When you experience deep loneliness, you are willing to give up everything in exchange for healing…people will be sent to you to mediate God's healing, and they will be able to offer you the deep sense of belonging that you desire and gives meaning to all you do." (Pp. 47-48)

Who were the people that God would provide to help me do this? What if I never found another person who could understand my agony, and truly *get it*? I was in Intensive Care. Who was going to take care of me? I had no idea that it would be an *army* of gay Christians, as well as gay people of other faiths.

Chapter Fourteen

JOURNAL ENTRIES

As I mentioned earlier, I began counseling in May 1997—just about three months after Anna's death. It was scary in some ways, yet comforting in others. The Lord provided me with a truly godly man, and I learned much from him. He is a rare person because he *gets it*. I believe this is the way God has gifted him.

One of my biggest challenges in counseling was to shed my legalistic view of God and try to understand His love and grace. Beginning with a very potent message at our church, I started to learn what legalism is and what it is not. Legalism is not avoiding a commitment to absolutes or to disciplines. Legalism pursues faith on a rules-oriented basis. It is a way of "keeping score" and it *appears* to offer safety and security. One reason that legalism is so deadly, is that it so closely resembles the real thing. At times, changing my view of God often seems like a hopeless task.

In another talk at our church, our pastor spoke of *hopeless* people. He said they tend to think the following about problems in life:

1. It will last forever (permanent)
2. It affects every area of my life (pervasive)
3. It is all my fault (personal)

Of course, this accurately described my thoughts about Anna's suicide.

As my counseling continued, I realized I had two *very* major hurdles I had to overcome: A) I couldn't trust God fully—or anyone else, and B) I was filled with fear.

I was afraid of losing my husband, my other daughter, my grandchildren, my parents, my siblings, my counselor, my ability to earn a living, my church, my home, and even, at times, my life.

Because of my legalistic upbringing, I knew almost nothing about the *Love* of God. I only knew His discipline and displeasure. This is how I raised Anna. Remember again with me what Anna told my Dad in the same month that she died; she had not gone to church for a long time because she had been taught that she was "dirty and useless." She thought that God was there with a big stick ready to hit her when she did something wrong. I understood that well, because when she died, I felt the same way.

About a month after I began therapy, I began to journal using the form of letters to my counselor. Here is where I would like to share my heart with you. And my heart still hurts.

Sunday, June 22, 1997

I still feel so confused about everything—about how I feel about God, about the lack of joy in my worship, about the difficulty I have praying. Sometimes I feel so guilty about not doing the things I used to do before Anna died—like cooking supper every night. I feel like it's somehow wrong for me to enjoy anything in the light of what had to have been unbearable pain for Anna. Anna was my "heartbeat" and I had such longing for her to come home and get her life straightened out and I prayed so long and faithfully for her and I feel that God just threw that prayer back in my face.

Saturday, June 28, 1997

It was 4 months ago today that Anna took her life, and 17 weeks ago today that we were making endless phone calls, making arrangements with a neighbor to care for our cat, talking with Anna's Dad by phone about funeral arrangements, trying to figure out what and how to pack, selling our living room furniture to strangers. Today—17 weeks later, it all seems so surrealistic. Today, it doesn't feel like my beautiful 29-year-old daughter is dead. How can this be? I have days like this now and then when it just doesn't seem real—but then I always know on THESE days that the "real" days will come. And I dread them. It hurts so bad on those days that sometimes I feel like I can't stand the pain.

Tuesday, July 15, 1997

I don't think I'm going to make it. It's too hard. I feel so totally alone. Where is the medication for this pain? I hate life. I don't want to live it. This pit I'm in is deep and dark and no one is volunteering to care for this bruised and bleeding human in intensive care. I feel like I've been run over by a train, then the train backed over me and ran over me again. Then someone called the city street crew and they came along with a shovel and threw me on the city trash heap.

Monday, July 28, 1997

I can't believe Anna's been gone 5 months. I haven't cried today, and it almost makes me feel disloyal to Anna. Grief is SO weird. I hate it! I'm sick of it! I'm sick of this roller coaster ride of emotions. I just looked up a verse in Job. It's Job 2:10b: "Shall we accept good from God and not trouble?"

Friday, August 1, 1997

Another horrible night, awake from 3:30-6:00 a.m. A year ago today, we put our 13-year-old cat to sleep. Anna was very upset that we would do this and called me a year ago tomorrow—the very last time I ever spoke to her, or heard her voice. When will this pain of being without her not hurt so bad?

August 28, 1997

Last night was rough. I kept thinking (and crying) about the horrendous pain Anna must have been in 6 months ago last night—so severe that she had to kill herself. Sometimes, I STILL can hardly believe it. I miss her unspeakably and feel so sad and broken about my own poor choices that contributed to her pain and inability to cope with life. That's something I'll have to live with forever. I wonder if I'll ever FEEL forgiven by God and I also wonder if it will ever be possible to forgive myself. How does one go about doing that?

August 30, 1997, Springfield

The closer we got to Springfield, the more sad and quiet and apprehensive I became. When we got into town, we stopped at a grocery store and I purchased a long-stemmed red rose and long-stemmed white rose and a piece of white ribbon—all to take to Anna's grave. It was and is excruciatingly painful to see the black granite stone with Anna's name and dates of her birth and death on it. I cried and cried. Then I asked Bob to get me a paper towel from the car trunk and I wiped all the cut grass from her stone. There was a faded American flag stuck in the ground, a pink rose (dead) and a beaded necklace lying on the stone.

I stuck my roses in the ground, we took some pictures, I cried some more and we left. It feels like I'm starting over with the grief—we are in the same place, with the same people and grieving the same death of our daughter (and sister), that we did 6 months ago. This afternoon, Nathan, Cheryl, Beckie, Bob and I went through Anna's boxes of things, about 10 or 12 of them. At times, it was very painful as I learned more and more of what had transpired in her life over the past few years. There are many papers, but I found no diary or journal. Although today was very hard, I feel a sense of peace and thankfulness at being allowed to go through her things.

Wednesday, September 17, 1997

[In this journal, there are Scripture verses printed on some of the pages—on this particular page, the verses are Psalms 51:1-2,7,10-12. "Have mercy on me, O God, according to your unfailing love; according to your great compassion blot out my transgressions. Wash away all my iniquity and cleanse me from my sin…Cleanse me with hyssop, and I will be clean; wash me, and I will be whiter than snow... Create in me a pure heart, O God, and renew a steadfast spirit within me. Do not cast me from your presence or take your Holy Spirit from me. Restore to me the joy of your salvation and grant me a willing spirit to sustain me."]

I just wanted to be sure to write something on THIS day, the day of "driving the stake"—a day I can look back on and know that I confessed my horrible sin that led to my daughter's death—and have been forgiven—and that you were witness to it. Thank you for praying with me. I pray that God will keep my heart tender always.

I feel a sense of sadness, but it is laced with a sense of peace tonight. What an awesome God we have!

Sunday, September 28, 1997

Seven months

Seven months she's gone
How can this possibly be?
It feels more like seven years
Or the seven days of the week
"If only" plagues my thoughts
Of things that might have been
If only I could confess
To her my gravest sin
I let her down, you see
When she was very young
And as a youthful parent
Left many things undone
I know that God forgives
That knowledge is in my head
I wonder when it will get
The distance to my heart instead
I thank God for a man named Steve
Who counsels me through this pain
Who helps me to function daily
And is teaching me to live again
He is Jesus "with skin on" to me
And many more things too besides
He always understands
No matter what I confide
Though at times I wish to die
Today, I choose to live
And pray that some day I'll have
Something meaningful to give

October 3, 1997

My Dearest Anna, You've been in heaven for 7 months and 5 days and I'm still struggling to understand why you chose to take your life. In fact, it was 31 weeks ago tonight that we received the call from you Dad telling us you were gone. Mostly, I feel nothing but the deep gnawing pain of having lost my first-born child. Sometimes I feel angry that you've put all of us through this kind of pain, but when I feel angry, I think of the pain YOU must have been in to do this drastic deed. How I wish I could have helped you, but then, you didn't want anything to do with me. Your last contact with me was the letter you wrote to me in early August 1996. At that time, everyone advised me to abide by your wishes and not try to contact you. A big part of me wishes I hadn't listened to anyone, not even myself. Over the past months, Anna, I've had to take a hard look at myself, and what things I did to you in your childhood that caused you to take this path. You and I were so alike I often called you my "heartbeat." We were both so sensitive and full of compassion for others. But unfortunately, my compassion for others circumvented you and left you out in the cold.

Sweetheart, I wish with all my heart that you could forgive me. I know you had figured out that I parented you as I was parented, using guilt and manipulation in so many different ways—ways that ultimately destroyed you. Even today, I'm trying to understand what love is, I love you and always have—but it must have seemed to you like I didn't love you. God is bringing many people and things (like books) into my life that are helping me understand myself better and that are teaching me how to behave better; but it's all coming too late for you. I am learning that when difficulties come into my life, I am responsible only for my REACTIONS to them, unless I have directly caused the difficulty. In your case, I not only directly caused some of your difficulties, but I also reacted badly to YOUR response to those difficulties. What a mess I made of your life!

I have many, many moments, hours and days when I want to join you, Sweetheart. But my motives are all wrong. I often wish to die so I can be with YOU, not so I can be with the Lord. It's so hard to have you gone. I still have all the cards and gifts I got for you between August 1996 and when you died. I was going to give you all those things. I don't think I'll ever get over the fact that you took your life during a period of time when you and I were estranged. I never got to tell you I loved you, and you thought I DIDN'T. I was so proud of you for so many things—your compassion for AIDS patients, your intelligence, your beauty, your musical talent, your ability to be a good friend to people. I wanted you to know that I am an HIV nurse—coordinator of a free HIV clinic. I never had the chance to tell you that. I only started the job 6 weeks before you died. Maybe somehow you know it anyway. Anna, sometimes I am completely overwhelmed with the number of poor choices I've made in life (those are the times I wish to do as you did), and how my poor choices so dramatically affected your life. With God's help, I am trying to make better choices from now on. Oh, I know I'll make more mistakes, but I pray that they will never be of such magnitude that they will cause such horrendous pain to another person. When you were a little girl, you were one of two very bright lights in my life (the other is your sister, Beckie). In many ways, Anna, you still are a bright light—but there's so much pain with it now. I love you, Anna.

November 28, 1997

To Anna

Nine months ago today
Your life on earth did end
I'm still so very sad
And wonder if my heart will mend.

There was another nine-month stretch
When you were inside of me
And I couldn't wait to find out

Just what kind of child you'd be

You were my first-born child
I longed for you so very much
I wanted to be your Mother
And shower you daily with love
I still miss you so very much
The pain is so hard to bear
And my hopes for you are gone
And my insides seem to tear
Your pain must have been so awful
To take your own life this way
You must have felt so hopeless
Was it because you were gay?

You said that I was self-centered
To a large extent, that's true
I wish, though, that you had known
How very much I loved you

You were such a beautiful person
For many years of your life
You gave of yourself to others
And yet, inside, there must have been strife

I know that you're at peace now
Resting at our Savior's feet
I know He's caring well for you
Until that Day when we shall meet

For now, though, I must learn
With memories to be content
With visions, dreams and pictures
And all that to me you have meant

I'm told the pain will always be
Lodged deeply within my heart
The pain of longing for you
And having to be apart

I will always love you, Anna
Your life flowed out from mine
I wanted only peace for you
And now you have it—a different kind

Saturday, February 28, 1998

Well, this first anniversary of Anna's death is almost over. It's really been hard and I cried several times. I don't honestly know if I'm capable of enduring any more pain. Only 2 people called today, my nephew and Don. Right now I really DO just want to give up. What's the point of this pain? Is it really drawing me to the Lord, or alienating me from Him? I guess I'll get through it somehow. I went through some of Anna's things today and re-read all the sympathy cards we've gotten over the past year. I just wanted to THINK about Anna. I miss her so much.

Thursday, March 5, 1998

I awakened this morning with the immediate thought, "A year ago today, I put my precious daughter into a hole in the ground." How can this be? I've heard it said that we all have a God-shaped vacuum in us that only He can fill. Today, I have an Anna-shaped vacuum in my heart. As I was getting ready for Anna's funeral a year ago now, I kept thinking, "I don't want to do this; I don't want to do this! Isn't there SOME WAY out of this???" I remember feeling like I wanted to run away.

Thursday, October 22, 1998—Anna's 31st birthday

I think Anna's birthday is more difficult this year than last. I read something in a nursing journal that said the second year of grief is worse than the first—because the reality sets in, and your support system drops away. How true! I read in my journal from this time last year. I got lots of cards and flowers from my brother, etc. I did get some cards from my family, and, would you believe flowers from Julio today. I keep hoping if I keep writing, I can climb out of this pit I'm in. I'm DONE. I sobbed most of the evening. My heart is so broken and my energy so depleted.

Wednesday, January 20, 1999

I'm wondering how much longer I can "do life." It's been a long time since I crashed like I did today. I wonder if I'll ever believe I'm a worthwhile person. The bottom line is that I'm not okay. I am in unbelievable emotional pain, and I don't fully understand why. Just 2 years ago, Anna was alive. I want her and my life back.

Friday, January 22, 1999

Dear God,

I don't understand you. I don't like you and I'm really angry with you. I feel very guilty about that. I'm waiting for you to strike me with yet another tragedy. Are all these tragedies my fault? A result of my poor choices? Did you really think the way to draw me closer to you and help me understand you and your supposed love, grace and mercy was to take Anna? How COULD you??!! I don't want anything to do with you. I can't read the Bible; I listened to no Christian radio today. I've "caught" myself talking to you today and stopped. You don't answer my prayers anyway. You seem to glibly allow people to die, who want to live, yet you ignore my prayer to take me because I WANT to die. WHY? I feel like you hate me, but I'm told you love me. What kind of "love" takes a mother's daughter by suicide during an estrangement? A little voice says you may want to use me to help others but I'd rather have Anna, thank you very much. Do YOU "get it?"

Saturday, January 23, 1999

Dear God,

Maybe my problem is that I keep trying to figure you out. Maybe that's pretty much an impossibility. I've read the Bible a lot since Anna died and numbers of Christian books. But none of that has really brought me any closer to understanding you. If a supposed friend of mine murdered my daughter, do you think I'd be able to love that person? Oh, the theologians would say I could do that, but only with your help. I read, I pray, I listen to Christian radio, music, tapes and go to church, all out of habit. I feel nothing for a God who has allowed so much pain in my life. I'm getting close to giving up.

February 28, 1999 Anna's death—2 years ago today

Today, my visual image is stuck on the fact that 2 years ago now, Anna was hanging from her closet bar—ALL DAY LONG—15 hours. I do so wish God would call me Home.

Sunday, January 9, 2000—My Dad's 88th birthday and his death date

It's so hard to believe my Dad is gone. We came home from their apartment less than two weeks ago. This will be a difficult week. Memorial Service in North Carolina, transferal of my Dad's body to St. Louis, driving my Mother to St. Louis, visitation, funeral and burial…the memories are already flooding in.

Saturday, January 15, 2000

Well, we buried my Dad today. The hardest part, by far, was taking our last look at him before the casket was closed. It has been a very difficult time, with many thoughts and remembrances of Anna, but few have said anything to me at all. After all, it's been almost 3 years. What can I expect?? I should be "over it" by now. NOT!!

Monday, February 28, 2000—Three years since Anna died

I am still alive, but only by God's grace. Why does this anniversary seem worse than the other two? Maybe because I had to work today and sit through a staff meeting and it all seemed so "trivial" compared to what has happened in my life in the last three years. Today, my poor choices have simply and completely wrung me out. I CAN'T start over. I CAN'T bring Anna back. But I'm not sure I can go on living with the enormity of what my poor choices have done—to others, as well as to me. Anna deserved better from her Mother. I don't even deserve the title "Mother."

February 28, 2000

Poem by Beckie—first poem she's ever written!

To Anna

It's been three years today since we said goodbye
And oh, the many tears that we cried
You left this world so suddenly
I guess you just needed to be free

The pain you held inside your heart
I could only imagine because now we're apart
I miss you so much and wish you were here
Because life isn't the same without you near

Our Daddy, how he loved you so
It was so hard for him to let you go
Our Mother, what a change she's made
But oh, how she wishes you had stayed
Not only to show you how much she cares
But to tell you she's sorry for the pain you did bear
Oh Anna, you meant the world to me
If I only could have made you see
That you were loved unconditionally
But that wasn't enough to set you free

Now we know you are in the sky
With our Lord and Savior, Jesus Christ
And one day we will be there, too
To tell you "hello" and how much we love you

So take good care up there in Heaven
We know you have many friends to share
The love you feel inside your heart
Even though we are still apart

I love you—Beckie

Chapter Fifteen

A COLLECTION OF IMPORTANT THOUGHTS

As my transformation continued, I found myself looking for a church that welcomes *and* affirms *and* celebrates same gender, monogamous, lifelong relationships. Our church was not that kind of church. Willow Creek Community Church welcomed all people, but taught that homosexual activity is a sin. We hung in there with them for about three years, but there was no movement toward Willow Creek becoming an "open and affirming" church. We met with the leaders and elders at the church, and they did not agree with us. So be it.

My own personal theory on large organizations which are built on millions of dollars, is that they would lose their funding if they welcomed and celebrated God's gay, lesbian, bisexual and transgender children. This includes organizations like Moody Bible Institute, Focus on the Family (James Dobson), Jerry Falwell's church and school, Pat Robertson's ministries, and D. James Kennedy, pastor of a very large church in Coral Gables, Florida. If Jerry Falwell's funding was threatened by his simply dining with us (since the Bible prohibits "dining with sinners") there is little hope, short of a miracle, that these multi-million dollar organizations are going to change their stance. We knew we had to and wanted to move on.

Peggy Campolo and Kathy Stayton attend an American Baptist Church in Wayne, Pennsylvania. The following is their church's covenant:

The Covenant of the Central Baptist Church—Wayne Pennsylvania

As a Community of Faith, we respond to the loving presence of God in our lives. We affirm Jesus Christ as the fullest expression of God in human life, the foundation for what we think, feel, and do.

We need each other. We accept each other. We are accountable to each other. We help one another discover the fullness of our humanity. We affirm and challenge one another, enriched by different beliefs and feelings about how God's love is made real.

We recognize the personal and communal need to cultivate our lives in the Spirit. We commit ourselves to deepen our understanding of what it means to be God's people. We covenant to engage in corporate worship, Bible study, prayer and meditation, group life, giving of resources and hearing those who suffer.

We reach out as a welcoming community of faith. We covenant as individuals and as a congregation to work with others toward peace, justice and the wholeness of God's creation.

Personally, I don't know how to take issue with those statements. Do you?

Recently, a brochure came across my desk at work, Fox Valley Community Church (an affiliate of Universal Fellowship of Metropolitan Community Churches). Their mission statement says:

> *The mission of Fox Valley Community Church is to extend God's diverse community beyond previously known boundaries through the Restoration, Transformation, Integration, and Activation of ourselves and our world.*

I especially appreciated the following statement in their brochure: "FVCC cannot be called a welcoming or affirming congregation. Those terms imply an outsider being welcomed into the fold. You are not an outsider here. Fellow explorers like you are building this church. We are all spiritual pilgrims on the road together."

And so, because of all this new information, I was attempting to get past the grid of my legalistic thinking and I became involved in WOW2000.

Their web site states:

> **WITNESS OUR WELCOME: GOD'S PROMISE IS FOR YOU!**
> *An historic ecumenical gathering of Welcoming Churches and their allies in the U.S. and Canada.*
>
> *Our Mission: We will gather as members and friends of the Welcoming Church Movement to worship, study and play. We will gather in our human diversity to celebrate God's love for all people of all sexual orientations. We will gather to experience the presence of Jesus Christ and participate in the Spirit's work to transform church and society.*
>
> *Sponsored by:*
> *Affirming Congregation Programme (United Church of Canada)*
> *Association of Welcoming and Affirming Baptists (American Baptist)*
> *More Light Presbyterians*
> *Open and Affirming Ministries (Disciples of Christ)*
> *Reconciling in Christ Program (Lutheran)*
> *Reconciling Congregation Program (United Methodist)*
> *Supportive Congregations Network (Brethren/Mennonite)*

Major Funding Provided by:
Broadway United Church of Christ (New York)
E. Rhodes and Leona B. Carpenter Foundation
First United Church of Oak Park (Illinois)

WOW2000 was held at Northern Illinois University in DeKalb, near our home, on August 3-6, 2000. When I learned of this event, I e-mailed the contact person, Mark Bowman. He lives in Chicago, and invited me to come to a planning session the end of January 2000. Bob and I went.

Until this meeting, I had only been a minority in a group of people one time, as part of my job. One of my patients, an African-American woman, who was HIV positive, was murdered. That in itself was such a painful thing for me. I went to her funeral, where I was the only white woman. I felt very uncomfortable.

At the WOW2000 planning meeting, I was again a minority. Bob and I were the only heterosexual couple in the room. I'll never forget one lady we met there. We had just come through the line to receive our cafeteria-style dinner, when this lady said to us, "Hi! I'm Cathryn Cummings-Bond. I don't believe I've met you!!" We introduced ourselves, and then went to different tables to eat. Cathryn is pastor of a church in the Seattle, Washington area.

After supper, at the beginning of the first planning session, the co-organizer, Jacki Belile, asked each of us to tell a little bit about ourselves and what we were expecting to come out of WOW2000.

When it was my turn, and I shared my story about Anna, very briefly, there was a sad murmur that rippled through the rest of the room.

The next day, at the second planning session, Cathryn came to us and handed us her business card, saying, "You guys go to such a big church. I'll bet you don't have a pastor you can readily call on when you need one." She was right. She then said, "I would like to be that person for you. Please call me anytime you need to." We were once again conscious of angels that God continues to send our way to watch over and care for us.

Cathryn also gave us a CD called, "Let Freedom Ring," recorded by a member of her church, Steve Peterson. She said to us "This CD will knock your socks off!" And she was right! Allow me to quote the words of two of the songs Steve wrote and sang:

Let Freedom Ring

In a western state, a bright young man was slain
Prejudice puts on a face, it has a name
But this wave of hate cannot put out the flame
For the truth that burns
within cannot be contained

chorus
Let freedom ring from the schools and churches
that teach ignorance and fear
Let freedom ring in the halls of Congress
with a message loud and clear
For the fear that used to chain us has
been changed to fearless pride
And the words they use to maim us
have become our battle cry
And we will not give up hope until
The last one is set free
And we can sing let freedom ring!

In a southern town, injustice strikes again
A man is hated for the color of his skin
But this time around we won't let hatred win
For intolerance can't match the
Love we feel within

(chorus)

So we stand here with our candle in the night
And we pray that somehow truth will be the light
That will someday end this wave of tyranny.
Until we all can live life honestly,
Then none of us is free

(chorus)

Walk A Mile

Walk a mile in these shoes,
walk a mile in these shoes
Before you criticize,
try a pair of these on for size
Walk a mile on this road,
Walk a mile with this load
You'll see a new point of view,
If you walk a mile in these shoes

It's so easy to point a finger,
it's so easy to criticize
But who are we, to throw the first stone
So before you go looking for sawdust
in somebody else's eyes
Take a look at yourself and take
the beam out of your own
Patience and understanding,
kindness and charity
Are things we all could use a little more of
So instead of condescending,
try a little empathy
Open your heart,
And show a deeper side to your love

(All words and music by Steve Peterson, Copyright 1999, Ironwood Studios, Vagrant Studios; Harmony Grove Music. P.O. Box 19214, Seattle Washington. All Rights Reserved)

As WOW2000 approached, I was asked to co-lead a workshop with Roberta Kreider, editor and compiler of *From Wounded Hearts* and *Together In Love.* The workshop was titled, *Building Good Relationships in Mixed Orientation Families.*

This was the first time I told my story since my beliefs about homosexuality had become completely transformed. The workshop was very well attended, and one young man, John Davis, e-mailed Roberta and me after the event and said he wanted to make a professional video of our stories! WOW! That dream became a reality about a year later. The video is entitled *"Family Stories: Journeys of Spirit in Mixed Orientation Families."* You can obtain a copy of it by contacting TEACH Project (www.teachproject.org).

Homophobia

Some time ago, something struck me as I re-read Anna's coming out letter. Anna had written, "I *want* to be gay," rather than "I *am* gay," or "I *am* a lesbian." It occurs to me that because of my extreme homophobia, which I learned from my family and my church, Anna herself was homophobic. She obviously had great difficulty coming out to herself and her self-hatred was complete in her final desperate act of suicide.

Later, I was to read a paper by Don and Carmen Bergman, entitled "Why We Cannot Heal Among You: An Open Letter to Our Christian Community." The Bergman's are Christian-Reformed believers who are parents of a gay son. They state that "the serious challenge is not how to square homosexuality with certain passages of the Bible that seem to condemn it, but rather how to reconcile rejection, prejudice and cruelty toward gays and their supporters—with the gracious, unconditional love of Christ."

In the last few years, I've come to realize that stereotypes stem from people's ignorance and sometimes they are just plain vicious, no matter to whom they are applied. We probably all have our own understanding of the word *stereotype*, but to me, in the case of GLBT people, it means that I think they are all the same, all believe the same way, and all do the same things. How ridiculously naïve of me! I believe that we must *never* stereotype anyone. No one should be *type-cast*. God has made each of us in His image, while at the same time, making each of us unique, and He loves each of us unconditionally. Of that, I am certain.

A word to family and friends
Many of you reading this book are friends or family members of a GLBT person. I would like to talk with you for a moment. Maybe you have rejected your loved one in the past. Maybe you still do. I would say to you, it is okay to feel what you feel. Every parent who mothers or fathers a child has hopes and dreams for that child. You imagine the day when your child will come to you with monumental news. "Mom, I got accepted to grad school." "Dad, I just got a big promotion at work." "Mom and Dad, I asked Laurie to marry me." But there are three words that most parents or other family and friends do not ever want to hear. Those words are: "*I am gay.*"

In our world today, there is a possibility that you *may* hear these words from a child, a sibling, a friend, or a church member. How will you handle this news? You need to know that all the emotions you experience when you receive the news that you have a gay loved one are "okay." I felt afraid, angry, confused, and sad. These emotions frequently bubbled to the surface. This is not wrong. Remember this: *feelings are not right or wrong. It is the manner of their expression that is either appropriate or inappropriate.* It is normal to worry about what other family members or friends will say and think. It is normal to worry about how our loved one will be treated in society and especially in the church. It is okay to be angry with God. He can take it. After all, He could have prevented all of this, right?

I remember praying that God would bring a special man into Anna's life. How many of you have prayed or do continue to pray like this? At the very least, you may pray that your loved one will remain celibate for the rest of their life. You may hope that they have the *decency* to not tell anyone else about their sexual orientation. You may be fearful about what others will say if they find out. I remember thinking, "I'd rather Anna be dead than gay." I felt so guilty about those feelings. Right after Anna came out, my sister sent me Barbara Johnson's book, *Where Does A Mother Go To Resign?* In the first chapter, Barbara says about her gay son what I was feeling: "I'd rather he be dead than gay." I found some comfort in knowing I was not alone. Neither are you alone. There are many out there who are experiencing what you are. The challenge is to find them because as heterosexual people, especially if we are Christ-followers, our tendency is to go under cover with the information of our loved one's homosexual orientation.

For a long time, after Anna came out of the closet, I did not tell *anyone.* I was too embarrassed and just plain scared.

Some years ago, we visited my nephew and his family who live in another state. This was a kind of "testing-the-waters" weekend with my side of the family, the legalistic group. We had decided not to come out to my nephew unless God opened the way. As Bob and I were preparing to go to bed that first night in their home, we didn't think the topic would come up. But God in His wisdom had a plan. The second evening of our visit, my nephew asked so many questions that I suspected he might have been corresponding with Beckie, who at the time was not supportive of our new beliefs. *Maybe she had tried to enlist her cousin's help to convince us to go back to the truth,* I thought.

Surprisingly, they had not talked. My nephew, who had been close to Anna and had taken part in her funeral, simply cared about what was going on in our lives. The challenge for us was to not overwhelm him with information, but to wait for him to ask questions, and allow some silences to just hang in mid-air. Of course, my nephew and his wife do not agree with us, but they made it clear that they love us and do not stand in judgment of us. They even said that they hope what we are doing will save some lives. Maybe there will be a reason for them to seek out more information. My nephew hinted that he might need to do some research on the topic. So, we continue to pray for them, and wait for them to ask us more questions.

A word to our GLBT family of choice

What happens if you are experiencing depression? This is likely *not* due to your sexual orientation, but due to the way you are treated *because* of your sexual orientation.

Rhea Murray, author of *A Journey To Moriah,* noticed that her son seemed depressed and sad. Because she suspected he might be gay, she took a huge step, and gave him a newspaper article about a support group for gay young people. She said to her son Bruce, "I think it's [the support group] a great idea! If you know anyone at school who can benefit from this information, why don't you pass it along to them?"

A few days later, this act of loving initiative allowed Bruce to courageously voice his own revelation about his homosexual orientation to his mom. Rhea says, "I felt surely my heart would break, so painful was it for me to witness my child's suffering. I told Bruce, 'You won't have to deal with this alone anymore. We'll handle it as a family from now on. We're in this together.'"

And I want to say to those of you reading this book right now, if you are experiencing depression, please see a counselor. I suffer from depression, I take medication, and saw a counselor weekly for six and one-half years. Do not shy away from avenues of help that are available to you. There are many wonderful counselors out there who are very supportive and ready to truly understand and help. Consider that *you* may educate your counselor, as I did mine. Sometimes I think *he* should pay *me*! (Not really. He has saved my life.)

IV

NEW LIFE

CHAPTER SIXTEEN

A PERSONAL WORD

Shortly after we returned home from Lynchburg in 1999, I e-mailed Mel White to thank him for paying our way for this life-changing weekend. He e-mailed back just three words: "DO YOUR HOMEWORK." And I did.

I began to understand that the Bible MUST be taken as a whole, within the context and culture of the day. Picking out a verse here and there to support what I think and believe is inappropriate. Actually, I have come to realize that the Bible, the inspired Word of God, may appear to say just about anything I want it to say. This was a real stretch for me, having been raised to believe that the Bible is "literally" translated, and as II Timothy 3:16 says, "All Scripture is given by inspiration of God, and is profitable for doctrine, reproof, instruction in righteousness."

It took a fair amount of time for me to understand that the "clobber passages" are gross misinterpretations, and are taken out of context and the culture of the day. ("Clobber passages" are those Bible verses frequently used to condemn homosexuality.) Tony Campolo states that if we take the verses in Leviticus that seem to condemn homosexuality literally, and ignore the culture of the day, then we must also take the other laws in Leviticus literally as well. Leviticus 11:7-8 states it is unlawful to eat pork, or touch the skin of a dead pig. Tony says, "Well, that just puts the whole Super Bowl thing in question."

Speaking of the "clobber passages," I had an interesting experience awhile back. I was asked to speak at a co-worker's Baptist church, during a weeklong prayer for healing of AIDS victims. I asked her what she wanted me to talk about and she told me anything I wanted to. I told her I was most comfortable sharing the story of Anna's death, and how my entire life had changed as a result of that. More than once, I made sure my co-worker knew what I was going to say. She said it would be okay. Well, it wasn't. I got about two-thirds of the way through my story, when the pastor of the church stood up and said, "You have one minute to finish, and then sit down." Needless to say, I became pretty unnerved, my mouth went totally dry, and I lamely finished with words along the lines of we all need to love people unconditionally, as Jesus does. After I sat down, the pastor did a 15-minute diatribe on the "clobber passages," prefacing his comments with, "I feel I need to correct some things that have just been said here." I wanted to fall into a hole.

My supervisor had come with me to the church. When I was dismissed and sat down, I whispered to her, "Can we leave now?" She said, "Yes, we can, but I prefer that we stay." We stayed. I went to the ladies room and had an abbreviated cry over my wounded feelings. My co-worker joined me there and was full of apologies and regrets about the way her pastor had handled the whole thing. The sad part was that I understood. Because I used to believe the same way he does.

Once I regained my composure, I found myself wishing I had asked this pastor (when he told me to sit down), if his suit was made of mixed cloth, or if he had shaved that morning, if he ever cut his sideburns or if he ever did work on the Sabbath—which, of course, are all cause for being put to death, according to Old Testament law. It's probably a good thing that I didn't think of that in the moment. Actually, what I really wanted to ask him was if he had ever had sex with his wife when she was having her period!

I would also like to include a note here about how my beliefs have changed regarding the passage in Romans. I am aware that some evangelicals discount the Old Testament laws, but base their beliefs about homosexuality on certain New Testament verses, particularly the passage in Romans 1:26-32. After having the Greek text of these verses explained to me, I understood that the people mentioned in this passage were heterosexual by orientation but were having same-gender sex, which of course was "unnatural" for them. But the passage that sent me literally running out of the den one morning and almost screaming, was Romans 1:29-31, which states: "They have become filled with envy, murder, strife, deceit and malice. They are gossips, slanderers, God-haters, insolent, arrogant and boastful; they invent ways of doing evil; they disobey their parents; they are senseless, faithless, heartless, ruthless..." Whoa! Wait just a minute here. I had met nearly 200 gay Christians in Lynchburg, and many, many more since then. I could never in a million years describe a single one of them as a "God-hater" or any of the other terms listed in this passage.

Two years after Anna's death, Bob and I took a month-long sabbatical from our jobs. We holed up in a tiny cabin on Bull Shoals Lake in northern central Arkansas to begin healing and reconnecting with God.

One day as I explored the shore of the lake, listening to a worship tape on my Walkman, I found myself picking my way through loose, slippery rocks along the shoreline. There was no sandy beach or grass. Just rocks. Suddenly, the path I thought I had seen just disappeared and as I picked my way along, the rocks became more and more treacherous. I began to panic. I was afraid to turn around because I knew what I had just experienced, but I was also too frightened to move forward into the unfamiliar. After screaming "Help!" to a boat far out on the lake, I began to pray for help. My screams were not being heard at all by those on the boat. But God heard them.

Unable to move forward or backward, I began to consider the possibility of scaling the hill before me—a forty-five degree angle. It looked like a straight-up cliff to me! Unsure of how far it was to the top, I was very uncertain as to whether I could even make it without falling back down, hitting my head on the rocks and tumbling into the lake, never to be seen again. (Yes, I am being melodramatic!) As I climbed the hill, the early morning dew made everything slippery, and the tree limbs and bushes that I tried to hold on to simply came loose in my hands.

That scary climb parallels my journey over very rocky ground toward a new understanding of homosexuality. I could not return to the *safe* solutions I had been taught all my life. That would simply keep me stuck in legalism and shaky scriptural interpretation. Nor could I follow those who acknowledge that sexual orientation is not a choice, but then claim that celibacy is the only honorable way to live before God. (I love what Dotti said to me once. She said, "I'll be celibate if you will!") It seemed I had reached a stalemate. I could go *up* but was not quite sure where the *top* would be. I was clearly aware that I could fall back down and hit my head on the rocks of bigotry and prejudice.

But as you know, because you are reading this book, I did choose to go *up*. I understood that this would mean a whole new set of beliefs! I was fully aware of the fact that it would be much safer to stay were I was. Though I had come to believe that homosexuality is not a choice, I was not completely certain if I was really ready to *buck the establishment*—the conservative Christian community which was my home—and state publicly that I believed same sex, monogamous relationships were celebrated by God. I wondered where God was leading. But I did not wonder long.

In July of 2000, I had begun to ask God for a small group of gay Christians who would like to meet weekly for a Bible Study, prayer, support and fellowship. That group became a reality just after the Labor Day weekend of 2000. We met weekly for 3 years. There were anywhere from 8-12 of us and many drove long distances to attend. These people were our dearest friends. Some still are, even though we moved from Illinois to Arkansas in October of 2003 to be closer to our kids and grandkids and to be close to some wonderful GLBT people introduced to us by Peggy Campolo.

CHAPTER SEVENTEEN

TEACH PROJECT

After a dozen or so speaking engagements, Bob and I considered establishing a not-for-profit corporation. It was a dream that we had. We did not know if it could ever be fulfilled. Some seeds had been planted by friends of ours at the end of 2001. We called an attorney and he wanted $2000 to set up the 501(c)3. Bob bought a $40 book on how to form a not-for-profit 501(c)3 corporation and tackled it by himself.

I'll never forget what happened while Bob and I were sitting at the breakfast table one Saturday morning in early 2002. We began to brainstorm, and started to just kick around a possible name for this corporation. We came up with the acronym—TEACH—(T.E.A.C.H.) To Educate About the Consequences of Homophobia. We decided to add the word "Ministries." Our dream fulfillment began with the founding of TEACH Ministries. On July 12, 2002, TEACH Ministries Articles of Incorporation were filed with the state of Illinois, and it officially became a "not-for-profit" 501(c)3 corporation. There was still a mountain of work to do before we received not-for-profit status with the IRS. Bob submitted the application to the IRS in early March of 2003. We received a letter from them, stating that the approval process could take up to 120 days. Imagine our surprise and thankfulness when we received our approval letter just three weeks later.

In late 2004, TEACH Ministries became TEACH Project, upon a recommendation from our board of directors. We realized that people in both the GLBT community and Christian communities mistakenly assumed that TEACH Ministries was yet another ex-gay ministry dedicated to changing homosexual orientation to heterosexual orientation. It was important that we avoid this misinterpretation of our mission. Also, by adopting the name TEACH Project we are now able to speak in venues where we had previously been unwelcome, such as public high schools and community groups.

As our web site was developed, we began to be contacted by more organizations wanting us to tell our story. As of January 2005, I have spoken 46 times in 14 states, and Bob has spoken five times in four states. Bob has been a great asset to our work by joining me in the question/

answer/comments time after my speeches.

Let me share just a few stories from these speaking engagements:

Dave Bishop

October 1999 to May 2004

In Lynchburg in October of 1999, we met a sweet man by the name of Dave Bishop. He lived in Salem, Oregon. He was a handsome man my age. Keep in mind that in October 1999, we had just barely started our journey to our current transformed thinking. During that Soulforce event, Dave heard me say not once, but three times, that I believed homosexual

activity was sinful. It's a wonder any of those dear gay people would even speak to me after that, but they did.

In August of 2001, when I spoke at the Evangelicals Concerned Western Region summer conference, ConnECtion, in Denver, Colorado, Dave Bishop was also there. After my talk, he came up to me and told me that when he read the ConnECtion conference brochure a few weeks earlier, and saw that I was to be a speaker he said to himself, "Oh no! Not her again!!"

After that, Dave and I developed a close bond. I will never forget one event that happened in Lynchburg in October 2002. I was standing in the foyer of the church where we were gathering, before going to the park for the Pride Festival. Dave came in a bit late, and saw me standing there. He put his arms around me, and laid his head on my shoulder and just sobbed and sobbed, saying "Why do they hate us so much?"

Tragically, soon after that, Dave developed lymphoma. In May 2004, he had a bone marrow transplant from his brother who was a perfect match. A couple of weeks after the transplant, his kidneys failed. On May 20, 2004, Dave married the love of his life, Rex Lampert. On May 21, 2004, Dave passed quietly away and went to be with his Lord and Savior. I miss him terribly. But I am sure he and Anna have already found one another and are cheering us on—down here in the "Shadowlands."

Love Welcomes All Conference—Austin, Texas

February 2003

At a Soulforce event in October 2002, our dear friend Jeff Lutes told us about a conference he was planning in Austin in February, 2003, called

Love Welcomes All. This conference was to be held across town from where another conference, sponsored by Focus on the Family and Dr. James Dobson was also being held. That conference was called *Love Won Out.* Jeff is a gay man, a psychotherapist, former Southern Baptist, committed Christian and partnered with Gary (who is deaf) for many years. Jeff and Gary adopted a little deaf boy from China. What a delight to be in their home and watch them raise this very precious little boy named Nikko!

Jeff asked me to come and tell my story at the *Love Welcomes All* conference. That was an amazing experience for Bob and me! I will always remember what one young man said to me after my talk: "My mother is across town at Dobson's conference, *Love Won Out,* and I do SO wish she would have been at this conference to hear your story." There were many similar comments.

This was a particularly exciting conference for me. The first edition of my book had just been printed and 100 copies were sent to me at the church via overnight mail. They arrived just as I finished my talk. We sold 42 copies in the first 20 minutes.

First Congregational Church
Ottawa, IL, March 2003

In March of 2003, I was invited to speak at the First Congregational Church in Ottawa, IL. This church was going through the process of considering becoming an Open and Affirming church. Their very wise pastor had led them through a series of studies during the Sunday school hour to help them understand the spiritual violence being perpetrated by religious policies of exclusion of GLBT people from most churches. In September of 2003, this pastor's dream was realized by a unanimous vote that their church become officially "open and affirming." What a joy for us to receive that news!

Cathedral of Hope
Dallas, Texas, and Oklahoma City, Oklahoma, May 2003

At the *Love Welcomes All* conference in Austin, Texas, we had the privilege of meeting The Rev. Dr. Mona West, who was the Senior Pastor at the Cathedral of Hope church in Dallas. I was surprised when I received an email from her, inviting me to come and tell my story at this very large church on Mother's Day.

That particular Sunday in May, I spoke three times—at two services on Sunday morning in Dallas, and an evening service at Cathedral of Hope, Oklahoma City in the evening. The morning services were attended by more than a thousand people! I was very nervous. The video *From Tragedy to Transformation* was borne out of that talk. The congregations were engaging and responsive audiences. By that time, I had built some humor into my talks, to lighten the atmosphere, and also to give me a chance to take a drink of water for my dry mouth. It was an amazing experience to sign more than a hundred of my books for people waiting in line after the services. Many times, I was asked to address my brief comments in the front of the book to the gay or lesbian person's parents. Did they read the book? Who knows?

That afternoon, we drove on to Oklahoma City, and spoke at the Cathedral of Hope. We realized that the audience has a great deal to do with the success of any talk! I had to give these people permission to laugh, and even then, they were unable to. There were some very wounded people in that church that evening.

Questioning Youth Centers
Naperville, Illinois, January 2004

Questioning Youth Centers (QYC) are support groups for young people ages 16-20 who are either gay, lesbian, bisexual, transgender, or are allies of GLBT youth.

I will always remember a particular evening. We were back in Illinois after having moved to Arkansas three months earlier. The temperature in Little Rock was sixty degrees when we left home. The night of this QYC meeting, the temperature was zero degrees, and I had a raging sinus infection. This event was held in the basement of a church. The kids were *rowdy;* in fact, they gave new meaning to the word *rowdy*! I did not think that they would settle down long enough to listen to me.

For the first time since I had been giving talks, I sat down in a chair. I was too weak to stand. I began to speak. Within less than two minutes, you could hear a pin drop on the floor of this room. Every student was silent and really *listening* to what I was saying, not just *hearing* my words. When I was finished, they clapped for a long time. They asked questions and made comments. Bob and I were astounded at the depth of their thought processes and their creativity. At the end of the evening, almost all of them came up to us and thanked us. Two more speaking engagements in high schools came out of that one event.

PFLAG Chapter—Brand New Chapter
Wheaton, IL, January 2004

Bob and I have come to love this non-profit organization—PFLAG—which stands for Parents, Families and Friends of Lesbians and Gays. I have spoken at a number of their chapters throughout the country. It was an honor to be asked to be the speaker at the very first meeting of this new chapter.

This particular PFLAG meeting was very important to me. Located in the city of Wheaton is a very conservative Christian college, Wheaton College. My mother and brother graduated from Wheaton College, my sister graduated from the nursing program affiliated with Wheaton College, I went to Wheaton College for one year and worked there for a little over a year. My newly found beliefs would be little more than heresy in that particular college environment.

I was surprised when forty Wheaton citizens showed up at this PFLAG meeting—many who had graduated from Wheaton College and who were also gay and lesbian. This seemed ironic and I felt somewhat "vindicated" with my current understanding of homosexuality. I am not sure I can explain why.

Many in this meeting wept as I spoke. After my talk, they all went around the room and gave their names (if comfortable doing so) and why they had come to this meeting. There were some very significant comments. I will never forget one in particular. A very handsome man in his early fifties, said, "My name is George, and this is the first time that I've ever admitted in public that I am a gay man." There were more tears, and for me, a thankfulness that this dear man was able to finally speak out loud who he really is!

PFLAG Meeting
Springfield, Missouri, May 2004

This story is near and dear to my heart. For a couple of years, I had known that I needed and wanted to go back to the town where Anna had lived and died, and apologize to Anna's friends. That became a reality in May of 2004, when I was invited to speak to the local PFLAG chapter in her town. The apprehension leading up to speaking at that meeting was excruciating. I had hoped some of Anna's friends would show up, but I was also scared to death that they *would*. I did not know how to prepare for their reactions to me, if any. I had worked and reworked my talk many times over.

Finally, the day came. I was a nervous wreck. It helped that my daughter Beckie introduced me with a wonderful speech of a few minutes, all of her own writing.

When we arrived at the meeting location, Bob and I were trying to figure out the seating in the small chapel. Beckie interrupted me and beckoned me to her and another lady. She said, "Mom, this is one of Anna's friends." [Her identity must remain anonymous.] My heart stopped and I felt my breath catch. I knew almost nothing about this lady except that she and Anna had been partners for a time, and at Anna's visitation and funeral, we moved her flowers away from the casket not once, but twice, and put flowers from my family in their place. Once, I even asked this woman and her children to leave the casket as they were blocking others from viewing Anna.

At this May PFLAG meeting, this dear lady wanted to talk with me in private. We went into the hallway, and she said to me, "I certainly hope that you are not planning to dishonor Anna's memory by making her suicide all about her being a lesbian. Do you deny that you abused her? That you sexually abused her?" Shocked nearly to silence, I told her, "I am well aware of the abuse Anna took from my lips and my looks, and my silence, and any other way I could find to make her feel guilty about her behavior, but I did not sexually or physically abuse her." This woman did not believe me. I began to cry, a rare occurrence before I speak, because I am always too nervous. I pleaded with her to stay and hear my talk, to hear me out. She had only planned to come long enough to confront me and say what she had to say and then leave. She finally agreed to stay and she sat in the front row.

I had built into this particular talk an apology, and request for forgiveness. Here is what I said: "Some of you have struggled long and hard. You have read many books and articles, and some of you may have even prayed that God would "heal" you of your homosexuality. Speaking of healing, I am aware that some of you here today knew Anna. Thank you for coming. I am also aware that it must be pretty hard to trust my words. In fact, you may think I've totally missed what Anna's suicide was about. I believe Anna told you that I abused her in every way—verbally, emotionally, physically and sexually. If that's what you believe, it would be nearly impossible to change your mind, and I won't try. I readily admit that I verbally and emotionally abused Anna. I did not physically or sexually abuse her, but it may have felt to her like I did. I ask for your forgiveness. If you are not able to do that yet, I hope you will someday find it in your heart to forgive me. I admit I don't deserve it, but that's the nature of forgiveness...it's a gift of freedom we don't deserve. I would also like to ask forgiveness for the way I treated many of you at Anna's visitation, funeral and burial. I am grateful for your presence here today."

I then finished my talk and opened it up for questions and comments. A few questions were asked, and then this dear lady, sitting in the front row, got up out of her chair, and walked toward me with tears streaming down her cheeks. She took both my hands in hers and said, "I forgive you. I forgive you." I thanked her and we held each for a moment as nearly forty people looked on. Many were crying, and so were we.

This is what miracles there are in my life.

International Film Festival
Provincetown, Massachusetts, June 2004

My husband, Bob, would like to share the following story:

> At ConnECtion in San Diego, California in 2003, Mary Lou and I met Jewel Jones, a lovely lesbian from Provincetown, Massachusetts. After that conference, we became fast friends. Jewel submitted Mary Lou's most recent video, **From Tragedy to Transformation** to the International Film Festival in Provincetown. It was accepted. What a thrill that was for all of us! Jewel worked very hard in that effort. She made arrangements for Mary Lou and me to travel to Provincetown to introduce the video, and to speak at a couple of churches on Cape Cod. Jewel asked me to make my speaking debut on Father's Day of this year at MCC Cape Cod.

> Jewel is a deeply committed Christ-follower involved in providing love and guidance to the gay community in Cape Cod. She and Peggy Campolo are co-founders of an organization known as **The Lighthouse: A Beacon of Hope**, and it is truly that. Jewel finds ways to connect with hurting GLBT folks on a regular basis. She is a strong prayer warrior as well, and has a strong vision to see GLBT people accepted in every area of our society.

Gay/Straight Alliance
Glen Ellyn, Illinois, January 2005

This speaking engagement came out of the QYC meeting mentioned earlier. To be invited into a high school to tell my story was miraculous, in our minds! There were young people from two other GSAs in the area; there were about forty kids and club sponsors.

I learned something very interesting from these young people. After my talks, I always open the floor for questions and comments. I tell the audience that no question is "out of bounds." They may ask us anything they want to. These kids asked questions for over an hour. One young lady, raised her hand and said, "I just want to know if you've gone back to that pastor of the Baptist church in Aurora who told you that you had one minute to finish and then sit down, and set him straight about his mistaken beliefs!" Then she asked, "Why haven't you told everyone in your family what you're doing now?" (I have not felt free to talk with my family, as they are all conservative Christians and would strongly disagree with what we do. For now, I prefer to simply have a good relationship with them. Many families have issues on which they disagree and mine is no exception. That's okay with me.) To this young lady's questions, I said, "Well, I might go back to that Baptist minister and maybe even my family, if you'll go with me." That brought laughter from the whole crowd.

Jason and DeMarco
Many places all over the country

At the *Love Welcomes All* conference in Austin, Texas in February of 2003, we were privileged to hear Jason and deMarco in concert for the very first time. Jason and deMarco are two young gay men who have the most amazing voices and singing/arranging talents. At the ages of 29 and 30, these two young men have touched our lives in a very special way. They are both committed Christ-followers, and they are committed to each other as life partners. I have a very special feeling about these young men. I honestly think they are the most important role models in our nation today. They are living proof and strong witnesses to the fact that young gay people *can and do* live in monogamous relationships. I believe that Jason and deMarco may stem the tide of the AIDS epidemic. Bob and I are honored to call these two young men our very dear friends.

Listen to their CDs. *Spirit Pop* and *Songs of the Spirit* are my two favorites.

You may purchase them through their web site:

www.jasonanddemarco.com.

A False Focus on My Family

Colorado Springs, Colorado, April 29 – May 2 2005

On the first of May, Soulforce went to Colorado Springs to bring truth in love to Dr. James Dobson, head of Focus on the Family. Dr. Dobson is a powerful, political Christian. Jeff Lutes (mentioned earlier) spent countless hours over the past 2 years preparing for this event. He wrote a booklet that is filled with incredible research, called *A False Focus on My Family: Why every person of faith should be deeply troubled by Dr. James Dobson's dangerous and misleading words about the lesbian, gay, bisexual, and transgender community.* Our Soulforce delegation planned to take a tour of the famous world headquarters of Focus on the Family. There was hope that Dr. Dobson would sit down with some of these fine families and attempt to understand that homosexual people may raise families just as heterosexual people do. Not only did that not happen, Focus on the Family *closed their facility* to tours by the public for the two days Soulforce was in town. The papers stated that the organization feared for the safety of their employees!! I wonder what made them think their employees would be in danger since Soulforce has been, is, and always will be a *non-violent* organization based on principles set forth by Ghandi, Martin Luther King, Jr., and Jesus Himself.

Jeff Lutes asked me to write a letter to Dr. Dobson. Check out the web site for this event: www.DearDrDobson.com.

Dear Dr. Dobson,

My name is Mary Lou Wallner. I am 59 years old, and recently moved from the Chicago area to the Little Rock, Arkansas area. I was raised in a very conservative fundamentalist church environment. My family was part of the Plymouth Brethren sect. We were taught many things that I did not and do not understand. We had to wear hats to "meeting" on Sunday. We couldn't wear makeup. We could cut our hair, but not short. Women could not speak in meetings where men were present. We had to be at "meeting" every time the door was open. We had closed communion.

Then I went to a Christian college and discovered there were other Christians in the world besides the Plymouth Brethren. It was then that I asked to "sit back" and not take communion at the church where I grew up, because none of my college friends would be allowed to take communion with me.

Then I married a guy from this Christian college. He was not Plymouth Brethren. My mother didn't even look at my engagement ring for 3 weeks. He and I were ultimately divorced after 12 years of marriage and the birth of 2 daughters.

In 1988, my oldest daughter, Anna, came out to us as a lesbian. She was also a Christian. I did not accept that in her and told her I would always love her but would forever hate "that," and would pray every day that she would change her mind and attitude. She did not.

You see, I raised my girls on Hide or Seek, Tough Love, etc. I believed you held all the answers to everything. I even went to a conference in Denver at a Nazarene Church where I listened to you and Joyce Landorf teach a wonderful seminar. I'll never forget you talking about your little boy who climbed up into a pickup truck bed and couldn't get down. You said that your little boy said quietly, "Somebody help the boy. Somebody help the boy."

I also raised my kids on Bill Gothard. I'll never forget my first husband spanking our youngest daughter when she was about three years old, until she "cried softly." She was also "bruised softly" on her bottom. This was supposed to break her will, not her spirit.

Today, my oldest daughter, the Christian lesbian, is dead. She committed suicide on February 28, 1997, by hanging herself from the bar in her closet at the age of 29. She left no note. It was at that time that I had to research the topic of homosexuality. After reading many books, and talking with people on both sides of the issue (including John Ortberg, Mel White, Phillip Yancey, Peggy Campolo and Dr. Gilbert Bilezekian), and studying the Scriptures, my husband and I finally understood that homosexuality is not a choice. We certainly do not promote promiscuity, but after getting to know hundreds of GLBT Christians, we realized that they did not choose their orientation, and if it wasn't chosen, how could it be a sin?

For me, largely due to the way I was raised and taught by the church, "different" somehow meant "bad." That is simply not true in any sense of the word. What on earth and in heaven would we do if we were all alike? That means that all but one of us is unnecessary. Regarding gays and lesbians, it is our observation that most of them consider their orientation a gift from God, and if we would get to know them better, we would find that they have a multitude of gifts to offer us!

In the Christian community, Dr. Dobson, who in their right mind would choose an orientation that would cause them to be abused, maligned, hated and even murdered?

I am part of Ralph Blair's organization called Evangelicals Concerned. I was a keynote speaker at their summer conference, ConnECtion, in Denver in 2001. Soon after that, I was given 3 other tapes of a previous ConnECtion—talks by Gil Moegherle. Dr. Dobson, I grew up on "Focus on the Family" broadcasts, with Gil Moegherle as your co-host. If what is written in his book, and spoken on his tape is true, you cannot possibly win your "war on America."

Where is Christ's unconditional love for all people in your message? Where is Christ's grace and salvation for any who accept Jesus, regardless of race, color, ethnic orientation or sexual orientation?

I used to receive your free magazine and newsletter. My wonderfully wise Dad, a Plymouth Brethren, finally cancelled all your materials from coming to their home because in his words, you had become way too "political." We did the same because of your judgment against homosexuals.

It seems to me that John Paulk speaks for himself, along with many other Exodus leaders. They all had to leave that ex-gay ministry because they were not converted to heterosexuals—and indeed were still homosexuals, and since they did not choose it, they could not change it!!

What would you do, Dr. Dobson, if your own unmarried daughter admitted to you that she is a lesbian? Just possibly, it would change the whole course of right-wing evangelical Christendom—for the better.

In my opinion, the church has created a "monster." We have singles groups in all our churches, for heterosexuals. But for homosexuals, we have nothing. I am an RN and was an HIV nurse for 5 ½ years. I believe that in part, the fundamental church of Jesus Christ is responsible for the AIDS epidemic. What do you think would happen if our churches (like the one where my husband and I were members for 7 years— Willow Creek Community Church) decided to embrace gays, lesbians, bisexuals and transgenders, and create singles groups for them?? Do you suppose we might be able to teach homosexuals about purity? About holiness? About monogamy?

My heart and soul grieves for you, Dr. Dobson, along with Dr. Falwell, Pat Robertson, D. James Kennedy and Dr. Joe Stowell. (We were casual friends with Joe and Martie Stowell, and Joe was the one who suggested I write a book. When I did, he refused to answer our phone calls or e-mails when he found out we were "dining with sinners" like Mel White.) Sadly, I know well what all five of you would have to lose should you declare your unconditional love for God's gay, lesbian, bisexual and transgender children: Millions and millions of dollars!!! How tragic to put money and huge organizations and mighty political power ahead of God's own children.

I echo the words of your small boy, Ryan. "Somebody help God's GLBT children. Somebody help these children whom Jesus loves and the church scorns." Dr. Dobson, will you be courageous enough to just meet with Mel White, with Peggy Campolo, with other Soulforce folks, with Ralph Blair?

When Soulforce comes to Colorado Springs next Spring, my husband and I will be there, and I will tell my story.

Would you have the courage to meet with my husband and me in private? That is and will be my prayer for the next many, many months.
To whoever reads this letter in Dr. Dobson's place, I ask you to have the courage to give it to Dr. Dobson and let him read it himself. I'm well aware that he is a very

busy man, but hopefully, he can spare 10 minutes to read this letter. Thank you.

In Christ's never-ending and always unconditional love,

Mary Lou Wallner
611 Dakota Dr.
Cabot, AR 72023
501-843-7121 home
501-743-1337 cell
e-mail: MaryLou@TEACHProject.org
web: www.TEACHProject.org

I was asked to say a few words at the Soulforce rally. Even though it was May 1st, it was very cold and there were snow flurries. Mel asked me to be brief because people were leaving the rally due to the cold temperature. Below is a brief excerpt from what I said:

Dr. Dobson… through a long and arduous journey my beliefs about homosexuality changed. I began to understand that it is not a choice—and if it is not a choice, then is it not a sin. There is much more to my story, but I desire to only issue a challenge to you: many times, people have asked what has most influenced us to change our beliefs. We cannot prescribe anyone else's journey, but we **urge** *these people to get to know gay Christians—I mean really know them—hear their stories and their pain. Witness their dedication to the Lord and to others.* **Dr. Dobson, I urge you to do the same. How can you do less?**

CHAPTER EIGHTEEN

CONCLUSION

The first time we went to Lynchburg, in October 1999, Mel White introduced me as a lady who "does not know *what* she believes about homosexuality." Today, my husband and I both know what we believe. We have heartfelt convictions that God honors same-sex, committed, monogamous, intimate partnerships. We celebrate these relationships with many dear friends.

When Soulforce went back to Lynchburg in October 2002, we paid our own way because we *wanted* to be there, and because Jerry Falwell had not toned down his anti-gay rhetoric. Soulforce held the first ever Pride Festival in a Lynchburg City park. I was one of several speakers.

There were hecklers with bullhorns saying things like, "You Sodomites! Repent or you'll burn in hell. If you die today, you're going to hell. You're all perverts." Some carried a huge banner that said, in black lettering, "Homosexuality Is A Sin." I was scheduled to speak late in the afternoon, and I argued with God up until that time. I said, "God, I cannot get up there and try to speak over these hecklers. I just can't do it!" I listened as Peggy Campolo spoke and trembled. She was almost shouted down, but she persisted and finished her speech. I thought, "I'm not nearly as strong as Peggy is." God continued to remind me that I had a much different story to tell than anyone else at the gathering. I paced and kept arguing with God. Finally, I asked Bob if he would stand before the crowd with me and give me moral support. As we approached the microphone, I prayed that God would put the words in my mouth that *He* wanted me to speak. I had not prepared anything, and here is what I said:

> *Four days ago would have been my daughter's 35th birthday. But she's dead. She committed suicide nearly six years ago. She was a Christian, and a lesbian, and I did not accept her sexual orientation. I did not love Anna unconditionally. Now she is dead, and I can do nothing to bring her back. Anna is dead because of the teachings I was taught by those of you at the top of the hill. My daughter is dead because of the untruth I was taught by the church. I am so thankful to now be at the bottom of the hill with my gay, lesbian, bisexual and transgender brothers and sisters. I love them dearly, and I know that God loves us just the way we are. Say it with me: GOD LOVES ME JUST THE WAY I AM. Say it again with me: GOD LOVES ME JUST THE WAY I AM.*

We left the microphone and returned to our seats on the hillside in the park. The Pride Festival ended, and Mel White came to us. He said, "Did you realize that soon after you started to speak about Anna, the hecklers stopped speaking altogether, and they never started again?" I had not been aware of their silence. I was aware only that God's presence in my life had given me the words to speak.

I have had many months to ponder what might have happened if Anna had lived. I once heard Joni Earickson Tada say, "Outside of the day of my conversion to Christ, the greatest gift from the Lord was my accident at Chesapeake Bay." That accident left her a quadriplegic. Anna's death will always be a tragedy. For the remainder of my life, I will cope with my many emotions about her suicide. Would I have embraced God's gay, lesbian, bisexual and transgender children if she had lived? I think not. Would I have researched homosexuality? Probably not. Would I have challenged my legalistic belief system? I doubt it. I have learned that God can be trusted with anything that comes into our lives. He can and will bring blessings out of disasters and sufferings. He is in the business of changing tragedies into triumphs and transforming us.

Once, I believed I would never begin to heal from Anna's tragic suicide. I could not believe Romans 8:28, that anything good could ever come from her death. Now, through God's grace and mercy, I *am* healing. The loss of Anna has transformed my entire belief system. My heart has been opened to a wonderful community of God's most precious children.

Anna took her life. She took it from herself and from me and from all her family members and friends. I do not know all the reasons she committed suicide. I am aware that because I did not love her unconditionally, and accept her lesbianism, I may have contributed to her tragic act.

I ask you, "Has God been faithful to me?" Yes, yes, yes! A thousand times, yes! We have an *awesome* God.

APPENDIX A

ANNA'S SONGS

All songs written and recorded by Anna between 1990 and 1996
Transcribed by Mary Lou Wallner, Anna's Mother, February 2000

MY CHILD'S SONG

I am here inside of you,
Do you know who I am?
Hidden in your deepest place,
Heal me if you can
I've been here so very long,
Won't you let me in?
If only you would listen,
You'd see how much I have to give
I'm a child, who lives within,
Who wants to run upon the land
Chasing butterflies and rainbows,
And playing in the sand
And I hold all your secrets,
All the feelings never shared
And I need for you to know me,
I need for you to care
You're the one inside of me,
I hear you call my name
But sometimes I'm so frightened,
I know you are in pain
All my life, I've pushed you away,
Afraid to let you in
How I need to feel you now,
Here I have to give
And together we can all do well
As we roam this beautiful land,
Creating butterflies and rainbows
In pictures on the sand
How I want to share your secrets,

Feel the feelings never expressed
For as I grow to know you,
I know that I am blessed
I'm the child inside of you,
Do you know who I am?
You're the child inside of me
You are who I am

WHERE DOES THE TIME GO

I see the butterflies winging on the wind
Perfect example of life that's born again
Sailing through the meadow that
All the plants may grow
Deep in its spirit, I wonder does it know
A circle of life is never broken
The souls of our beings intertwined
So oft the words are left unspoken
And we will find that we've been left behind
Where does the time go?
I watch their lives pass before me
Each moment precious in itself
Yet colored with the pain of knowing
A world, I'd rather hear of something else
Do you know the meaning of the passion?
Don't you know the truth we all are one?
Do you let them go without communion?
And finding that you've missed
The chance to know,
You watch them turn to gold
Where does the time go?
I see the butterflies winging on the wind
I feel their precious lives flow
Through me again
Sailing through this cluttered world
That all that touch me grow
Teaching us to find the strength
Inside that we may know

The circle of life is never broken
The souls of our being intertwined
Don't ever leave the things you feel unspoken
For you may find that you've been left behind
Don't let the time go
Where does the time go?

DO YOU KNOW ME

Each day I go to work, I wonder
How well you think you know me
What you ought to do and say
Would it change the way you see me?
Just when I think I'd be comfortable with you
All of a sudden the fear is back, brand new
Tell me why does it have to be this way
Why should I have to wonder?
Whether or not you'll stay
And be right there,
If you really know all about me
Every time we talk about our lives
I shy away from you
Avoiding the personal questions
I never share all I'd like to share with you
Sometimes I get so angry I can't even cry
Feel like I have to live my life as a lie,
When all I really want to do
Is to share my love with you
Say, will you share your love with me?
Well, if it's happened before
It can happen again
If I share with you
Will I lose my friend?
I don't know if I can do that one more time
But then I suppose if I want to be close
I will take the risk and let you know me
And maybe, just maybe, it'll be all right
Next time I tell somebody

It'll be easier to believe
I think I can be honest,
And I'll ask you to be free
So that, each day I go to work
I won't have to worry if you know me too well
Maybe each day I go to work,
I could have a friend there to support me
Right now, each day I go to work
I wonder how well you think you know me

CHILDREN OF LIGHT

I see the children sleeping
And I wonder what they're dreaming
Their innocence is wide-eyed
I hear the children playing
And a small voice inside of me is saying,
Play with me, too, play with me, too
I need to know you
But the violation of that night
Has brought my child's pain to light
Sometimes I just have to go away
Until I look at you
'Cause when I look at you,
I see your innocence
And I smile, and I'm thankful,
Yes, thankful for your love
Somehow the child in you
Has reached and touched the child in me
And shown me that the darkness fades away
My innocence is light
My innocence is light
And I feel I'm playing on a dream
And none of them the children I've seen
Remembering, remembering,
Always remembering
The children of the light
The children of the light

We're beautiful, loving,
Innocent children of the light
We're beautiful, loving,
Innocent children of the light

FINDING REST

Have you watched the river flow to the open sea?
Ever watch the changing tide on a sandy beach
Feeling the spirit move to
Show me what I've missed
Hear the voice of peace whisper, Rest
Where have I been, lost in my world
So far away struggling with the words
I quit listening, quit hearing a still small voice
Of your love, in my soul
I feel once again, winds are changing my life
Oh, show me; please show me how to get on
It seems as though you've surrounded me
With soul drenched in your light
And I'm feeling that I'm
Finally and truly not alone
As I ever watch the river flow to the open sea
And ever feel the changing
Tides flowing within me
Feeling the Spirit move,
To show me I am blessed
I hear the voice of peace
Whisper, whisper, Rest

SAVE THE BATTERED CHILD

A child gets home from
School to a raging inferno
His parents are screaming
The violence is teeming
A child in all of his innocence

Just wants to stop the fighting
Stepping into the midst of it
He becomes like a lightning rod
The angry cries, the hatred flies
The child is beaten down
Taking lifetimes of punishment
Never making a sound
Where is the justice?
How could he trust again?
One more child has been murdered
One more murderer is free to live
And he has hardly paid for what he did
How many children
Must suffer for these crimes?
Will we ever change the system?
Will the law ever be on their side?
Or do we have to watch more children die?
There's a young girl sitting in her room
She is frightened and alone
She knows she carries within her
A child that must never be known
Is there anyone she can run to?
When the pains begin inside
So there's no one there to rescue her
No one to hear her cry
And she's all alone as she loses
Her father's child
Her father's child
How many more children
Must suffer for these crimes?
Will we ever change the system?
Will the law ever be on their side?
Will it help us save the battered child?
The battered child
Save the battered child

FRAGMENTS

Just because you think you know me

Doesn't mean you have the right to touch me
Just because I'm close at hand
Don't think I'll be your sacrificial lamb
Just because you say you love me
Doesn't take away how much you've hurt me
Now your words are trite and empty
Do you think that I don't understand?
That they're meant to appease and deceive me?
I don't believe you anymore
Don't pretend your touch is gentle
Don't pretend your voice is kind
Every time you touch me
You rip away what's mine
It was mine to hold
It was mine to cherish
It was mine to give
And now there's nothing left
But fragments of my soul
I watched you walk away
Like nothing ever happened
I'm left with secrets that I cannot even find
Hidden in the fragments of my mind
The fragments of my mind
The fragments of my mind

THE MIRROR

I look in the mirror now
And wonder who is looking back at me
I think maybe I've heard your voice
Tell me now, who can you be?
And why do you frighten me?
I look in the mirror now
And wonder who's looking back at me
I don't recognize the eyes
You seem so far removed from me
So full of pain and misery
Why do you frighten me?
Tears roll down my face

Memories I can't seem to embrace
Loneliness crowded with activity
Drenched in this unfamiliarity
Surrounded by terror and anxiety
Why do you frighten me?
Oh, how you frighten me
I look in the mirror now
And wonder who is looking back at me
I look in the mirror now

THE PARTING

There were papers, presentations, and readings,
Oh God! The readings!
And lectures we've had to sit through
We've hassled with class schedules
And practicum hours, and parking
All for those three initials of M.S.W.
I remember the first time I saw all your faces
And tried to remember your names
I was scared to death, we all were
Wondering if we'd make it
Yet, look! Here we are today
There are so many people
Who've helped us on our journey
Together we've walked a special path
But the path has branched
Out in many directions
And we must go our separate ways
So let me take this time now
To share all my thanks
For all that I've learned through your eyes
Your passion for people
And learning of yourselves
Has helped me to recognize
And though we're at a crossroads
And we must say goodbye
We're blessed by each other as we go
For this is the time to celebrate the lives

Of those that we've come to know
Celebrate, celebrate with tears and laughter
Celebrate, celebrate the journey of our lives
For in knowing you,
I've come to know myself better,
But I have to say, I cannot tell a lie
It doesn't make it any easier to say goodbye
Remember your passion for people and yourselves
Even though today we say goodbye

APPENDIX B

RESOURCE LIST

Following is a list of resources that may be helpful to you as you educate yourself about the consequences of homophobia.

BOOKS AND PERIODICALS

Aarons, Leroy. *Prayers for Bobby: A Mother's Coming to Terms with the Suicide of Her Gay Son*. San Francisco: Harper, 1995.

Alexander, Marilyn Bennett and James Preston. *We Were Baptized Too: Claiming God's Grace for Lesbians and Gays.* Louisville, KY: Westminster John Knox Press, 1996.

Barbo, Beverly. *The Walking Wounded: A Mother's True Story of Her Son's Homosexuality and His Eventual AIDS Related Death!* Lindsborg, KS: Carlsons, 1987.

Barnett, Walter. *Homosexuality and the Bible: An Interpretation.* Wallingford, PA: Pendle Hill Publications, Pamphlet #226, 1979.

Bess, Rev. Howard H. *Pastor, I am Gay.* Palmer, Alaska: Palmer Publishing Co., 1995.

Blair, Dr. Ralph. *Homosexuality: Faith, Facts, and Fairy Tales.* New York: Evangelicals Concerned, 1991. Contains two messages given to a United Methodist Church.

Borhek, Mary V. *Coming Out to Parents.* 1983; Cleveland, Ohio: The Pilgrim Press, revised and updated, 1993.

Borhek, Mary V. *My Son Eric.* Cleveland, Ohio: The Pilgrim Press, 1979.

Boswell, John. *Christianity, Social Tolerance, and Homosexuality: Gay People in Western Europe from the Beginning of the Christian Era to the Fourteenth Century*. Chicago: The University of Chicago Press, 1980.

Bourassa, Kevin and Joe Varnell. *Just Married.* Madison, WI: The University of Wisconsin Press, 2002.

Brawley, Robert L., editor. *Biblical Ethics and Homosexuality: Listening to Scripture*. March 1996.

Buxton, Amity Pierce, Ph.D. *The Other Side of the Closet: The Coming Out Crisis for Straight Spouses.* Santa Monica, CA: IBS Press, Inc., 1991. Not written from a Christian viewpoint.

Cantwell, Mary Ann. *Homosexuality: The Secret a Child Dare Not Tell.* San Rafael, CA: Rafael Press, 1996.

Celebration of Same-Gender Covenants: Task Force Report. Pullen Memorial Baptist Church, Raleigh, North Carolina. April 1993. Also two audio cassettes: The Pullen Story-ECWR. Rev. Silver, and Pat Long.

Christians and Homosexuality: Dancing Toward the Light. Special issue of *The Other Side* magazine, 300 W. Apsley, Philadelphia, PA, 1994.

Cole, Beverly. *Cleaning Closets: A Mother's Story.* St. Louis, MO: Chalice Press, 1995.

Comstock, Gary David. *Gay Theology without Apology.* Cleveland, OH: The Pilgrim Press, 1993.

Cook, Ann Thompson. *And God Loves Each One.* Washington, D.C.: Task Force on Reconciliation, Dumbarton United Methodist Church, 1988, 1990.

Dew, Robb Forman. *The Family Heart: A Memoir of When Our Son Came Out.* New York, NY. Ballantine Books, a division of Random House, Inc., 1994

Empereur, James L. *Spiritual Direction and the Gay Person.* Continuum Publishing Group, 1998.

England, Michael E. *The Bible and Homosexuality*. 5th ed. Gaithersburg, MD: Chi Rho Press, 1988.

Fairchild, Betty and Nancy Hayward. *Now That You Know: What Every Parent Should Know About Homosexuality.* Orlando, FL: Harcourt Brace Jovanovich Publishers, 1989, 1979.

Ford, Michael. *Wounded Prophet: A Portrait of Henri J.M. Nouwen.* Doubleday, 1999.

Frontain, Raymond-Jean (introduction). *Reclaiming the Sacred: The Bible in Gay and Lesbian Culture.* Harrington Park Press, 1997.

Glaser, Chris. *Come Home! Reclaiming Spirituality and Community as Gay Men and Lesbians*, 2nd ed. Gaithersburg, MD: Chi Rho Press, 1988.

Glaser, Chris. *Coming Out as Sacrament.* Geneva Press, 1998.

Glaser, Chris. *The Word Is Out: Daily Reflections on the Bible for Lesbians and Gay Men*. Louisville, KY: Westminster John Knox Press, 1999.

Glaser, Chris. *Uncommon Calling: A Gay Christian's Struggle to Serve the Church*. Louisville, KY: Westminster John Knox Press, 1988.

Griffin, Carolyn Welch, Marlan J. Wirth and Arthur G. Wirth. *Beyond Acceptance: Parents of Lesbians & Gays Talk About Their Experiences.* New York, NY: St. Marten's Press, 1996.

Hazel, Dann. *Witness: Gay and Lesbian Clergy, Report from the Front.* Louisville, KY: Westminster John Knox Press, 1999.

Helminiak, Daniel A., Ph.D. *What the Bible Really Says About Homosexuality*. Millennium Edition Updated and Expanded. Alamo Square Press, April 2000.

Hershberger, Anne Krabill, editor. *Sexuality: God's Gift.* Scottdale, PA: Herald Press, 1999.

Hill, Leslie. *Marriage: A Spiritual Leading For Lesbian, Gay, and Straight Couples.* Wallingford, PA: Pendle Hill Publications, Pamphlet #308, 1993.

Hilton, Bruce. *Can Homophobia Be Cured? Wrestling with Questions that Challenge the Church*. Nashville, TN: Abingdon Press, 1992.

Johnston, Maury. *Gays Under Grace.* Winston-Derek Publishers, 1990.

Jordan, Mark D. *The Invention of Sodomy in Christian Theology* (The Chicago Series on Sexuality, History and Society). Chicago: University of Chicago Press, 1998.

Kreider, Roberta Showalter. *From Wounded Hearts: Faith Stories of Lesbian, Gay, Bisexual and Transgendered People and Those Who Love Them*. Gaithersburg, MD: Chi Rho Press, 1998.

Kreider, Roberta Showalter: *Together in Love: Faith Stories of Gay, Lesbian, Bisexual and Transgender Couples.* Kulpsville, PA: Published in association with Strategic Press, 2002.

Lutes, Jeff: *A False Focus on My Family: Why every person of faith should be deeply troubled by Dr. James Dobson's dangerous and misleading words about the lesbian, gay, bisexual, and transgendered community*. Thirty page booklet citing five Violent Claims from Dr. James Dobson, Founder and Executive Director of Focus on the Family, Colorado Springs, CO. Order through Soulforce website: www. soulforce.org.

Marcus, Eric. *Is It a Choice? Answers to 300 of the Most Frequently Asked Questions About Gays and Lesbians*: San Francisco: Harper/San Francisco, 1993.

McNaught, Brian. *Now That I'm Out, What Do I Do?* St. Martin's Press, 1998.

McNaught, Brian. *On Being Gay: Thoughts on Family, Faith and Love*. St. Martin's Press, 1989.

McNeill, John J. *Taking a Chance on God: Liberating Theology for Gays, Lesbians, and Their Lovers, Families and Friends.* Beacon Press, 1996.

McNeill, John J. *The Church and The Homosexual.* Beacon Press, 1993.

Morrison, Melanie. *The Grace of Coming Home: Spirituality, Sexuality, and the Struggle for Justice*. Cleveland, Ohio: The Pilgrim Press, 1995.

Murray, Rhea. *A Journey to Moriah.* Banta & Pool Literary Properties, LLC: 1020 Greenwood Avenue, Bloomington, IN 47401 1998. E-mail: writerpool@aol.com

Piazza, Michael S. *Holy Homosexuals: The Truth About Being Gay or Lesbian and Christian.* 2nd ed. Dallas, TX: The Sources of Hope Publishing House, 1995.

Polaski, LeDayne McLeese and Millard Eiland, editors. *Rightly Dividing the Word of Truth: A Resource for Congregations in Dialogue on Sexual Orientation*. Baptist Peace Fellowship of North America, 4800 Wedgewood Dr., Charlotte, NC 28210. (704) 521-6051.

E-mail: bpfna@bpfna.org. Also The Alliance of Baptists, 1328 Sixteenth
St. NW, Washington, DC 20036. (202) 745-7609. E-mail: AllianceofBap
tists@compuserve.com

Reverend Mel White: Family Values With Soul. Special issue of
Alternative Family magazine. P.O. Box 5650, River Forest, IL
60305-5650. Phone: (708) 386-4770. Fax: (708) 386-5662. E-mail:
info@altfammag.com. Web site: www.altfammag.com.

Samuel, Rev. Kader. **Openly Gay, Openly Christian: How the Bible
Really is Gay Friendly.** Leyland Publications, 1999.

Scanzoni, Letha and Virginia Ramey Mollenkott. **Is the Homosexual
My Neighbor? Another Christian View** (1978). **A Positive Christian
Response** (1994). San Francisco: Harper & Row, 1978, 1994.

Schoenhals, Rev. Robert. **The Scriptures and Homosexuality: A
Study of Biblical Texts.** Pamphlet. To obtain, write to: Rev. Robert
Schoenhals, Wesley Foundation at the University of Michigan, 602 E.
Huron, Ann Arbor, Michigan 48104-1594.

Scroggs, Robin. **The New Testament and Homosexuality.** Philadelphia:
Fortress Press, 1983.

Seow, C.L., editor. **Homosexuality and Christian Community.**
Louisville, KY: Westminster John Knox Press, 1996.

Siker, Jeffrey S. **Homosexuality in the Church: Both Sides of the
Debate.** 1994.

Spahr, Jane Adams, et al, editors. **Called OUT! The Voices and
Gifts of Lesbian, Gay, Bisexual, and Transgendered Presbyterians.**
Gaithersburg, MD: Chi Rho Press, 1995.

Stuart, Elizabeth, et al. **Religion is a Queer Thing: A Guide to the
Christian Faith for Lesbian, Gay, Bisexual and Transgendered
Persons.** Cleveland, OH: The Pilgrim Press, 1998.

Sweasey, Peter. **From Queer to Eternity: Spirituality in the Lives of
Lesbian, Gay and Bisexual People.** Cassell Academic, 1997.

Switzer, David K. **Coming Out As Parents.** Louisville, KY: Westminster
John Knox Press, 1996.

Switzer, David K. and John Thornburg. **Pastoral Care of Gays,
Lesbians and Their Families.** Philadelphia: Fortress Press, 1999.

"The Slow Miracle of Transformation." Article in *The Other Side* magazine, 300 W. Apsley, Philadelphia, PA, 1994.

March/April 2001 issue

Thorson-Smith, Sylvia. *Reconciling The Broken Silence: The Church in Dialogue on Gay and Lesbian Issues.* Louisville, KY: Published by the Christian Education Program Area of the Congregational Ministry Division, Presbyterian Church U.S.A., 1993.

Tigert, Leanne McCall. *Coming Out While Staying In: Struggles and Celebrations of Lesbians, Gays, and Bisexuals in the Church*. United Church Press, 1998.

Truluck, Rembert, *Steps to Recovery from Bible Abuse.* Chi Rho Press, 2000

Wallace, Kim, *Erik and Isabelle: Freshman Year at Foresthill High.* Sacramento, CA: Foglight Press, 2004.

Wallner, Mary Lou, *The Slow Miracle of Transformation.* Self-published through Trafford Publishing, Victoria, BC, Canada. Available through www.TEACHProject.org.

Waun, Maurine C. *More Than Welcome: Learning to Embrace Gay, Lesbian, Bisexual and Transgendered Persons in the Church*. C B P Press, 1999.

White, Mel. *Stranger At The Gate: To Be Gay and Christian in America*. New York: Simon & Shuster, 1994.

White, Mel. *What the Bible Says—and Doesn't Say—about Homosexuality.* Pamphlet. Order through Soulforce, Inc., P.O. Box 3195, Lynchburg, VA 24503, or info@soulforce.org, or www.soulforce.org.

Williams, Dorothy, editor. *The Church Studies Homosexuality: A Study for United Methodist Groups*. Nashville, TN: Cokesbury Press, 1994.

Wink, Walter. *Homosexuality and the Bible*. A booklet of an earlier version of this article that appeared in the *Christian Century Magazine, Christian Century Foundation, 1979.* Revised version, 1996 by Walter Wink.

Wink, Walter, editor. *Homosexuality and Christian Faith: Questions of*

Conscience for the Churches. Minneapolis, MN: Fortress Press, 1999.

Woog, Dan. ***Friends and Family: True Stories of Gay America's Straight Allies***. Consortium Book Sales and Distributors, 1999.

Yancey, Philip. ***What's So Amazing About Grace?*** Grand Rapids, MI: Zondervan Publishing House, 1997.

CASSETTES/VIDEOS/DVDs/CDs

Alexander-Moegerle, Gil. ***"James Dobson's War on America."*** Evangelicals Concerned Western Region, 1993. Tape #199803. Gil Moegerle started Focus on the Family with James Dobson. This tape gives an honest inside look at Dobson and his damaging politics.

Campolo, Peggy. ***"Straight But Not Narrow."*** Keynote Address, Evangelicals Concerned Western Region, 1994. Write to Peggy Campolo, P.O. Box 565, Wayne, PA 19087-0565.

Campolo, Tony and Peggy. ***"Two Sides of a Christian View of Homosexuality."*** North Park University Chapel, Feb. 29, 1996. Write to Tony and Peggy Campolo, P.O. Box 565, Wayne, PA 19087-0565.

Campolo, Tony and Peggy. ***"Living With Our Differences."*** American Baptist Churches of the Northwest Biennial. ***"Through A Glass Darkly."*** Sermon by Peggy Campolo at First Baptist Church, Birmingham, Michigan, April 21, 1996. Write to Tony and Peggy Campolo, P.O. Box 565, Wayne, PA 19087-0565.

Anna's Songs. A collection of 9 songs written by Mary Lou Wallner's Christian lesbian daughter who committed suicide on February 28, 1997. All are original compositions sung and played by Anna. Order through www.TEACHProject.org. Cost is $10 plus $2 shipping and handling.

Body of Dissent: Lesbian and Gay Mennonites and Brethren Continue the Journey. (39 min.) Toronto: Bridge Video Productions, 1994. Personal stories of lesbian and gay people from Mennonite and Brethren backgrounds. Available from BMC, P.O. Box 6300, Minneapolis, MN 55406-0300. (612) 722-6906. E-mail: BMCouncil@aol.com

Family Stories: Journeys of Spirit in Mixed Orientation Families.

156   THE SLOW MIRACLE OF TRANSFORMATION

(24 minutes). Foreword by Dr. Peter Gomes, Harvard University. Personal stories of Roberta Kreider, editor of *From Wounded Hearts: Faith Stories of Lesbians, Gays, Bisexual and Transgendered People and Those Who Love Them*, featuring Mary Lou Wallner and Roberta Kreider. Order through www.TEACHProject.org. Cost is $20 plus $2 shipping and handling.

Fish Can't Fly: Conversations about GOD and struggling to be Gay. (83 minutes), by Tom Murray. A documentary film available on DVD from http://www.fishcantfly.com

From Tragedy to Transformation. (30 minutes). Mary Lou Wallner's talk at Cathedral of Hope, Dallas, TX, Mother's Day 2003. Order through www.TEACHProject.org. Cost is $20 plus $2 shipping and handling.

Homosexuality: The Debate is Over: The Verdict is In: It's Not a Sickness, Not a Sin. Order through Soulforce website: www.soulforce.org. Cost is $25.

How Can I Be Sure God Loves Me Too? (23 min.), ***The Rhetoric of Intolerance*** (29 min.), and ***The Trials of Jimmy Creech*** (28 min.). Three messages by Mel White on one video. ($6.00) Available from Dubose McLane, 500 East Marilyn Avenue, Apartment E-75, State College, PA 16801-6267. Telephone: (814) 231-8318. E-mail: foxdaler@juno.com

Homosexuality and the Bible, by Rev. Ken Martin. A comprehensive and scholarly presentation available through MCC of Austin, TX at http://www.mccaustin.com from Rev. Martin at revkmartin@aol.com

Marsha Stevens Live in Concert. (Part 1, 59 min. - Part 2, 36 min. - Total, 95 min.). Costa Mesa. CA: BALM Publishing, 1993. Marsha Stevens, who wrote and composed the song, "For Those Tears I Died," when she was 16 years old, presents 14 songs that were written by her and composed with the aid of others from the Universal Fellowship of Metropolitan Community Churches. She also shares anecdotes and her personal story of being a lesbian woman of faith. Available from BALM Publishing, P.O. Box 1981, Costa Mesa, CA 92628.

Songs of the Spirit and ***Spirit Pop:*** Two of many musical CDs produced by Jason Warner and deMarco deCiccio. To order, view web site: www.jasonanddemarco.com.

Straight From the Heart: A Journey to Understanding and Love. (24 min.). Woman Vision Productions, 1994. Stories of parents' journeys to a new understanding of their gay and lesbian children. Available from Motivational Media, c/o PFLAG, Pittsburgh, P.O. Box 54, Verona, PA 15147. (412) 363-8839.

The Trials of Jimmy Creech. (28 min.) A dramatic interview with a heterosexual United Methodist clergyman who risked everything to support GLBT people and to end the policies that caricature and condemn them. Order through Soulforce website: www.soulforce.org. Cost is $15.

The Power of Youth. (18 min.) Jake Reitan, Soulforce Young Adult Director, uses dramatic historic footage to demonstrate the power of youthful activism. He explains simply and clearly the work of Soulforce and invites viewers to join. Order through Soulforce website: www.soulforce.org. Cost is $15.

There's A Wideness In God's Mercy. (30 min.), Dr. Lewis Smedes on Romans 1. Introduction by The Rev. Dr. Mel White, Founder, Executive Director of Soulforce, P.O. Box 3195, Lynchburg, VA 24503. Okay to copy or broadcast. Order through Soulforce website: www.soulforce.org. Cost is $15.

Two Sides of a Christian View of Homosexuality. (50 min.). Tony and Peggy Campolo speaking in North Park College Chapel, Thursday, Feb. 29, 1996. ($10.00). Available from North Park University, 3225 West Foster, Chicago, IL 60625. Contact person: Bill Hartley. (773) 244-5579.

ORGANIZATIONS and WEB SITES

Brethren/Mennonite Council for Lesbian and Gay Concerns (BMC), Jim Sauder, Executive Director, P.O. Box 6300, Minneapolis, MN 55406-0300. (612) 722-6906.

E-mail: BMCouncil@aol.com. Web site: http://www.webcom.com/bmc/.

Clergy United for the Equality of Homosexuals: P.O. Box 1831, Camarillo, CA 93011. (805) 484-6887.

Web site: www.clergyunited.com. E-mail: info@clergyunited.com

Connecting Families, Ruth Conrad Liechty, Contact Person, 1922 Cheryl Street, Goshen, IN 46526. (219) 533-5837. E-mail: rliechty@juno.com

Web site: www.DearDrDobson.com. Tells about Soulforce action in Colorado Springs, CO in May of 2005.

Evangelicals Concerned, Inc., 311 East 72nd St., New York, NY 10021. (212) 517-3161.

E-mail: ecincnyc@aol.com.

Evangelicals Concerned Western Region. P.O. Box 19734, Seattle, WA 98109-6734. (206) 621-8960.

Web site: www.ECWR.org.

Web site: www.graceonline.org. . A "Central" location where users and visitors alike can quickly find sources of churches, ministries, and businesses within the Christian community that appreciate the distinctive message that God gave to the Apostle Paul.

IMPACT Communications. Dotti Berry. Born to coach...the light in me sees the light in you!

Web site: www.GLBTcoach.com. E-mail: dotti@GLBTcoach.com.

Parents, Families, and Friends of Lesbians and Gays (PFLAG), 1012 Fourteenth Street, NW, #700, Washington, D.C. 20005. (202) 638-4200. E-mail: pflagdc@aol.com. or www.pflag.org

RJN Music, 8033 Sunset Blvd. Ste. 574, Hollywood, CA 93046. Web site: www.jasonanddemarco.com E-mail: rjnmusic@aol.com.

Soulforce, Inc. P.O. Box 3195, Lynchburg, VA 24503, (877) 705-6393. E-mail: RevMel@aol.com

Web site: www.soulforce.org.

TEACH Project (To Educate About the Consequences of Homophobia). Also TEACH Ministries. Founded in 2001 by Bob and Mary Lou Wallner.

Web site: www.TEACHProject.org . E-mail: info@TEACHProject.org

Universal Fellowship of Metropolitan Community Churches, 8704 Santa Monica Blvd., 2nd Floor, West Hollywood, CA 90069. (310) 360-

8640. Fax: (310) 360-8680.

E-mail: UFMCCHQ@aol.com.

Whosoever Magazine. Web site: www.whosoever.org. The
Reverend Candace Chellew. *'God Bless America!': Locating
Human Freedom in the Social Order* – http://www.whosoever.
org/v7i1/godbless.html

For I know the plans I have for you,
declares the Lord,
plans to prosper you and not to harm you,
plans to give you hope and a future.
—Jeremiah 29:11

Yet this I call to mind
and therefore I have hope;
Because of the Lord's great love
We are not consumed,
For His compassions never fail.
They are new every morning;
Great is Your faithfulness.
—Lamentations 3:21-23

Therefore, my dear brothers,
Stand firm, let nothing move you.
Always give yourselves fully
To the work of the Lord,
Because you know that your labor
In the Lord is not in vain.
—I Corinthians 15:58